MELVILLE

MANIFESTOS

THE
DEATH
OF
MEDIA

DANNY SCHECHTER

THE DEATH OF MEDIA

AND THE FIGHT TO SAVE DEMOCRACY

MELVILLE HOUSE PUBLISHING
HOBOKEN, NEW JERSEY

©2005 DANNY SCHECHTER

BOOK DESIGN: DAVID KONOPKA

MELVILLE HOUSE PUBLISHING
P.O. BOX 3278
HOBOKEN, NJ 07030

FIRST MELVILLE HOUSE PRINTING
ISBN: 0-9766583-6-4

PRINTED IN CANADA

LIBRARY OF CONGRESS CATALOGING-IN-PUBLICATION DATA

SCHECHTER, DANNY.
    THE DEATH OF MEDIA AND THE FIGHT TO SAVE DEMOCRACY / BY DANNY
SCHECHTER.
        P. CM.
    ISBN-13: 978-0-9766583-6-8
    ISBN-10: 0-9766583-6-4
    1. MASS MEDIA—POLITICAL ASPECTS—UNITED STATES. 2. JOURNALISM
—POLITICAL ASPECTS—UNITED STATES. 3. DEMOCRACY—UNITED STATES.
I. TITLE.
P95.82.U6S337 2005
302.23'0973—DC22

                                                    2005023043

CONTENTS

THE DEATH OF MEDIA

For a journalism of courage,
and a media system worthy of it

PART I

THE LAST DAYS OF OLD MEDIA

WHEN MEDIA UNDERMINES DEMOCRACY

American democracy is at risk. Our freedoms are threatened. Our political process is in danger. Sound the alarm.

For years, warnings like this have appeared in our media. Sometimes they are shouted at us in thundering editorials. Often they have tried to persuade us in reasoned columns and commentaries, raging at political turns of events with onerous implications. This is what the media is for, to serve as a fire bell in the night, a guardian and watchdog.

The founders of the American experiment in self-rule conferred a constitutional mandate on the media by assuring the rights of a free press. The courts have *mostly* upheld it. "Paramount among the responsibilities of a free press is the duty to prevent any part of the government from deceiving the people," wrote Supreme Court Justice Hugo L. Black.

That's the theory anyway.

Words like "duty" and "responsibility" seem oddly quaint today, as if they are throwbacks to an earlier time, in what was, perhaps, another country. Today, many of our most trenchant critics warn that the most serious threat to democracy is coming from the very press charged with protecting it.

Put simply: Our media is undermining democracy, and in some ways they have displaced it with a "mediaocracy"—rule by the agenda-setting power of privately owned media corporations. Unfortunately, this is one headline rarely in the news.

Not just liberals, but conservatives like Edward Luttwak realize this too, asking at a 2004 Arts and Ideas Festival at Yale, "can democracy survive the media?" He and other critics point to the lack of diversity of viewpoint in news reporting and shrinking substantive issue-oriented coverage during elections. They note that the focus on polls and personalities leads to what media critics call "agenda cutting," that is, weaning the public off of factual issues and policy choices and, by doing so, depoliticizing politics. The result is growing cynicism and many dropping out of politics altogether.

So concludes Roland Schatz of Media Tenor, a media firm that studies political coverage in many different countries: "The people's reaction to this is to turn their backs on the ballot boxes. The party of non-voters has grown to become the most important group in all Western democracies, a fact that has not been given sufficient attention by the media." That may be because it is the media itself that is encouraging this anti-democratic trend.

There are libraries full of very good books documenting how this has happened. Most explain how market logic tends to drive out public interest obligations. They show through case studies and well-documented narratives how news has been sanitized, journalists censored, and important stories suppressed. They have described a merger of news business and show business in an era of growing concentration of ownership that has led to a "dumbing down" of content. They decry packaging over substance and claim that we are in a "post journalism" era where information is a commodity but facts no longer matter.

They describe the ever-increasing transformation of the news into a corporate commodity. Thoughtful newspaper editors like Jon Carroll fear that corporate ownership is eroding the quality of our newspapers, telling an interviewer: "Newspaper-owning corporations—and I mean all of them, not just my own employer—have an unwritten pact with Wall Street that requires unsustainably high profit levels. Each year, newspapers shed reporters, editors, photographers, designers, and news whole. Each year, readers get less. Each year many of those readers turn elsewhere for their news."

Media workers, especially journalists, know how seductive this corporate pressure and, its corollary, creeping personal co-optation, can be. Most feel they have few means of resistance. "This is the deepest censorship of the self," writes the critic John Leonard, "an upward mobility and a downward trajectory."

Even media moguls like CNN founder Ted Turner now admit that big media is a threat to providing Americans with the news we need. Writing in the *Washington Monthly*, he turns on the industry he was once part of. He writes, "These big companies are not antagonistic; they do billions of dollars in business with each other. They don't compete; they cooperate to inhibit competition. You and I have both felt the impact. I felt it in 1981, when CBS, NBC, and ABC all came together to try to keep CNN from covering the White House. You've felt the impact over the past two years, as you saw little news from ABC, CBS, NBC, MSNBC, Fox, or CNN on the FCC's [Federal Communications Commission] actions. In early 2003, the Pew Research Center found that 72 percent of Americans had heard 'nothing at all' about the proposed FCC rule changes. Why? One never knows for sure, but it must have been clear to news directors that the more they covered this issue, the harder it would be for their corporate bosses to get the policy result they wanted. A few media conglomerates now exercise a near-monopoly over television news."

On the occasion of CNN's 25th anniversary in June 2005 Turner told a reunion of staffers that he yearned for a "return to a little more international coverage on the domestic feed and a little more environmental coverage and, maybe, a little less of the pervert of the day."

At a time when technology permits robust communication and citizen participation, big media has tended to become more hierarchal and top-down. Profit making has become its primary mission and its programming is often designed to maximize that goal and that goal alone. Its method is monologue, not dialogue, even as new gimmicks, including audience voting by phone and Internet chat, provide the illusion of viewer involvement.

If these domineering trends are leading to the domination of the mass media by a small cartel of giant corporate conglomerates, the emergence of new technologies and the growing awareness of a need for other voices has made an energetic and more diverse news media more viable. Early on in the history of TV it was decided that TV receivers would be cheap, but broadcast equipment prohibitively expensive. Now, with new affordable technology, a complete reversal of that traditional content distribution structure is possible.

There's a media war underway between the old school of newspapers, radio stations, and TV News and a new school of Internet-driven information— the web's satirical, culturally biting programming, podcasts, broadband new media, and blogs, literally millions of blogs. And now with audio blogging and video blogging emerging along with low-powered radio, Internet TV is soon to follow. For years media reformers have had the means of making their critique. Now they are finally getting the means of distributing it. This is turning the top-down, big media model on its head.

One of the most thoughtful bloggers, Juan Cole, a professor of History at the University of Michigan and an Iraq expert, responded to one critic by contrasting the independent spirit of blogging with the more controlled and sanitized environment of mainstream media, a.k.a., MSM: "The difference is that we are not under the constraints of making a 15% profit.... If we were the mainstream media (MSM, perhaps better thought of as corporate media), we would care if you threatened to stop reading us. Because although we might be professional news people, we would have the misfortune to be working for corporations that are mainly about making money. We would be ordered to try to avoid saying anything too controversial (and I don't mean 'Crossfire' controversial), because we would be calculating what would bring in 15% profits per annum on our operating capital. Would hours and hours of television 'reportage' and discussion of Michael Jackson or of Terri Schiavo or Scott Peterson (remember?) bring in viewers and advertising dollars? Then that is what we would be giving the public. Bread and circuses."

As society fragments along demographic lines and political differences, there's been a much commented-upon political polarization, but there has also been a far less-noticed cultural divide. On

American television, a right-wing campaign to denigrate the never-very-liberal media is used as a tactic to build audiences for Fox News and conservative-dominated talk radio. Its strategists know that in the absence of real competition on the left, viewers can be lured to outlets offering extreme and simplistic diatribes if they are wrapped in patriotism and populist rhetoric. The result is that viewers turn to media outlets they think they agree with—but perhaps not necessarily because they espouse conservative values so much as because these outlets express their estrangement from middle of the road politics.

The campaign to discredit centrist and liberal media has had an effect largely through repetitive attacks by politicians and pundits on what was unfairly branded "the liberalmediaelite." (John Podhoretz, the journalist credited with coining the phrase, later admitted he made it up because it played well with the conservative base, not because it was true.) This media bashing campaign, echoed on talk radio and news panel shows, has had its intended effect.

A 2005 State of Media Study found: "The public's evaluations of media credibility are more divided along ideological and partisan lines. Republicans have become more distrustful of virtually all major media outlets over the past four years, while Democratic evaluations of the news media have been mostly unchanged. As a result, only about half as many Republicans as Democrats rate a variety of well-known news outlets as credible, a list that includes ABC News, CBS News, NBC News, NPR, PBS's *NewsHour with Jim Lehrer*, the *New York Times*, *Newsweek*, *Time*, and *U.S. News and World Report*.

A Pew Center study confirmed this, noting: "Credibility ratings for the major broadcast and cable television outlets have fallen somewhat in recent years, due in large part to increased cynicism toward the media on the part of Republicans and conservatives. CNN no longer enjoys the top spot as the most credible TV news source; it is now in a statistical tie with CBS's *60 Minutes*. From 1996 to 2002, CNN was viewed as the most believable broadcast or cable outlet, but its ratings have fallen gradually over time. Today 32% of those able to rate CNN say they can believe all or most of what they see on the cable network. This is down from 37% in 2002, 39% in 2000, and a high of 42%."

Ironically, more progressive media critics were, in the same period, lambasting major media outlets for not being liberal at all, or even liberal enough, as they ignored economic gaps and downplayed issues of gender, class, and race. They complained that there were more news programs but less real news. Their more critical voices were soon heard only at university seminars or in the journalism reviews. Their critique of the mainstream turning into a mud stream was largely ignored on the broadcast spectrum or relegated to programs with small audiences.

At the same time, the commercial news industry was reformulating the news with shorter story counts, less overseas reporting, and shortened story length. As content became shallower, presentation became more cluttered. What was so liberal with the spread of show biz values, and celebrity? Nothing of course—but this labeling became part of the political polarization of the period, a process used to build large audiences on the basis of identity and ideology.

Soon there was less and less "hard news" in the news overall. Traditionally, "hard news" refers to coverage of international affairs, politics, and events in Washington, local government, and business and finance. Pew reported: "A smaller group of news consumers, less than a third of the public (31%), consistently focuses on these types of stories. At the other end of the spectrum, about one-in-ten Americans (13%) do not follow these subjects at all, preferring other kinds of news or no news at all. Over the past eight years, the hard news audience has ranged in size from a low of 24% in 2000 to its current level of 31%, with the increase over the past four years driven largely by the rise in interest in international news. While a minority overall, these hard news enthusiasts make up a majority of the audience for a number of news programs, and express distinctly different attitudes and preferences about what they want in the news."

This problem has become our challenge.

The challenge of media reformers is not just to critique the logic behind this system but also to envision an alternative, and then, where possible, build it. That's what some of our most creative software designers are doing with open source technology. That's what low cost documentary filmmakers are doing, helped by a small army of video and TV producers. They are not only attacking the media system but also becoming a new media.

As so much of mainstream media devolves into a mud stream, old media is losing its grip and appeal. We are in a transition period, but its outlines and possibilities are often more clear to visionaries than ordinary readers and computer users. Alternative media is also facing the challenge of coming up with business models that make it more sustainable.

There is now a growing citizens' movement that insists that the public has a right to expect more from the media and, in fact, has a right to receive better media. Media rights? Now that's a new concept. And in fact, in 2005 hundreds of organizations embraced a Bill of Media Rights.

This Bill of Media Rights, written by Jonathan Rintels with input from a coalition of media organizations, states: "According to the Supreme Court, the First Amendment protects the American public's right to 'an uninhibited marketplace of ideas in which truth will prevail' and to 'suitable access to social, political, aesthetic, moral and other ideas and experiences.' Moreover, it insists that it is 'the rights of the viewers and listeners, not the right of the broadcasters, which is paramount.' "

What are the rights of viewers and listeners? Stay tuned—but for now, we need to examine why the present system acts as if viewers and listeners have no rights.

THE PROBLEM OF CONTROL

I grew up in a world of three principal TV networks. Now there are hundreds of channels owned in large part by four principal networks and a handful of other media companies. Digital cable and satellite stations are all competing by offering endless channels and choices. But when you look closely, you find only a handful of companies controlling those cable systems and other conduits. All are driven by the market logic of the bottom line.

And that control has been documented. The top four broadcast networks may have a direct ownership interest in only 25% of the 102 broadcast channels, but, as public interest lawyer Marc Cooper of the Consumer Federation of America observed in testimony before Congress, "They have guaranteed access to distribution platforms on television and cable as well as close interconnection through stock ownership and joint ventures with the cable companies that control the remainder of the channels. The joint activities of this cabal has resulted in a video programming market that is a tight oligopoly by all traditional measures of market structure."

Talk of "market structure" or any economic framework like this is missing in most media discussions. Issues get attention but corporate interests rarely do. Few critics examine how decisions about programming, and even the structure and content of news shows, are influenced by a need to insure and advance the parent company's financial interests.

Ironically, concerns about the decline of informed debate in the media has paralleled the growing power and penetration of media. What's missing is called "viewpoint diversity," says Cooper.

This is a convoluted way of saying that companies that own the conduit control its content, preferring programming that reflects their values and interests, and all is aimed at doing well in the marketplace. They don't necessarily mind using shows from many producers as long as their costs can be controlled and profits maximized. What this leads to in real terms is a uniformity of genres and a dominance of entertainment-oriented shows that often have little to do with the public interest. Indeed they stifle localism and a full range of viewpoints.

This does not necessarily mean that entertainment programming is trivial. Well-elaborated plots, storylines, and characters often do a better job of treating social issues than flatter and less well-funded fact-based programs. The irony is that, in some instances, police dramas or shows like *ER* or *The Sopranos* give far more sophisticated insights into human behavior and political controversies than news and pseudo-documentary shows.

Media historian Robert McChesney—long one of the leading intellectuals trying to understand what's wrong with our media, as well as one of the leading activists trying to change it—reduces much of the media problem to this ownership dynamic and to the idea that media concentration breeds more commercialization and less public discourse. "The American media system is spinning out of control in a hyper-commercialized frenzy," writes McChesney. "Fewer than ten transnational media conglomerates dominate much of our media; fewer than two dozen account for the overwhelming majority of our newspapers, magazines, films, television, radio, and books. With every aspect of our media culture now fair game for commercial exploitation, we can look forward to the full-scale commercialization of sports, arts, and education, the disappearance of notions of public service from public discourse, and the degeneration of journalism, political coverage, and children's programming under commercial pressure."

This is true, yet it only scratches the surface of the deeper challenge. When you look back to the time when we had few networks and more diversified ownership, there was still no golden age of democratic media pluralism. Many of the corporate owners shared an ideological outlook. They were loyal to their interests and to those of their advertisers first. The media was often sycophantic to power, hostile to labor, insensitive to minorities, and contemptuous of cultural diversity.

Happily, throughout our history there has been a vibrant tradition of dissent, counter-media, and alternative presses. For example, there were 1,200 Socialist newspapers in America in 1912, run mostly by immigrants. Back then, Edward A. Ross wrote of much of the media of his day: "There is just one deadly damming count against the daily newspaper as it is coming to be, namely, *it does not give the news.* For all its pretensions, many a daily newspaper is not 'giving the public what it wants.' In spite of these widely trumpeted prodigies of costly 'journalistic enterprise,' these ferreting reporters and hurrying correspondents, these leased cables and special trains, news, good 'live' news, 'red-hot stuff' is deliberately being suppressed or distorted. This occurs oftener now than formerly and bids fair to occur yet oftener in the future."

This is prophetic, for clearly our problem is not a new one. Fortunately, there *is* something new to help us deal with it, namely, the Internet— offering the most revolutionary range of new alternative media since the invention of the printing press, offering thousands of websites with every possible viewpoint. For remaking the media system requires more than dismantling monopolies. It demands a lively and compellingly presented new culture of participatory media that offers different content and promotes citizenship, not consumerism.

We will never have the kind of democratic media system we need until the public is more aware of the current media's defects and opts into the process of both demanding changes and creating new channels of discourse. Ultimately, our media challenge is not just about "them," but about us, and what kind of media we can create and are prepared to fight for and take part in.

WATCHING DOESN'T MEAN LIKING

It's a mistake to believe that because people watch what's on TV, they like what they see. In media, as in politics, we choose among the choices we are given. It's not surprising that highly produced and well-marketed entertainment shows draw bigger audiences than comparatively lower budget news and documentary programming that lacks star appeal, advertising, and, more critically, on-air promotion.

The masters of media packaging know this, which is why many thirty-second TV commercials cost more than the shows they are broadcast in. Engineering audience interest is itself a science and an art, tapping the creativity and enterprise of advertising professionals.

Our current media is a sales platform, doing more selling than telling. It's powerful and seductive and highly engineered, through focus groups and the like, to attract and keep audiences by using humor, dramatic story telling, and hyped up news. It understands that its audiences want and need distractions and diversions from problem-plagued lives and overwork. (Americans have less leisure time than people in any Western country on earth. Economist Juliet Schor writes in *The Overworked American* that, "the average American today spends 1,949 hours at his or her job. This is 163 hours more than in 1969 and is equal nearly to a whole month of added work in a year.")

This does not mean that the media is just a tool for manipulation—its biggest product is itself, and most of it devotees find pleasure in its offerings. Watching television becomes a habit, a "plug-in drug" in the words of one critic. TV addiction is more pervasive than any other, especially frightening as the programs people watch also program them—influencing their worldview and what they think matters, what they should buy, and whom they should admire. TV doesn't just market products. It markets a culture that is presented as far more affluent than it is. And its greatest achievement is in not calling undue attention to its techniques. Media guru Marshall McLuhan understood this when he wrote that TV is "pervasively invisible" and does not call attention to its impact. It is just there—like a piece of living room furniture, or an appliance. Perhaps that's why Reagan era FCC Commissioner Mark Fowler compared TV to a "toaster with pictures."

At the same time, an industry that says it prides itself on "giving the people what they want" is now going through a major transition, because it has discovered that many people don't want what they are being given. You can only determine what people really want when they have real choice. Though perhaps this disconnect from their viewers' desire for real choice hasn't bothered broadcasters until it is too late because their programs exist to sell eyeballs to advertisers, not information to viewers.

Thus, although our media system is very powerful, invasive, and pervasive, it is also fragile, fragmented, and failing, even in its own terms. Just as there is a law of gravity, there are laws of history. Nothing lasts forever. Empires come and empires go. It seemed ironic that in an effort to attract religious viewers, media companies in 2005 began airing films about biblical prophecies concerning the "last days" as if they had some special exemption from the profound changes they were hyping.

We are at the end of an era, the end of media as we have known it.

THE LAST DAYS

I am not the only one with the feeling that we are living in the last days of our media system. Ten years ago, the writer Michael Crichton predicted the "extinction" of mass media in an introduction to the 1995 edition of *Project Censored* (an annual collection of downplayed and suppressed stories). The author of *Jurassic Park* said he wanted to focus on another "dinosaur" on the "road to extinction": "I am referring to the American media. And I use the term extinction literally. To my mind, it is likely that what we now understand as the mass media will be gone within the next ten years. Vanished without a trace."

While his prediction may have been off by a few years, he saw what others at the time didn't, essentially predicting the changes we are now witnessing—more viewers watching cable than network, the growth of satellite channels, a dramatic decline of newspaper circulation, the rise of the Internet, and the proliferation of diverse content, not to mention search engines and the bloggers and other new digital technologies.

Novelist Bruce Sterling has been tracking the death of media, too. He wrote his own call, the "Dead Media" manifesto (Deadmedia.org) about it, also drawing on dinosaur metaphors. "Our culture is experiencing a profound radiation of new species of media. The centralized, dinosaurian one-too-many media that roared and trampled through the 20th century are poorly adapted to the postmodern technological environment. The new media environment is warm with lumbering toothy digital mammals. It's all lynxes here, and gophers there, plus big fat venomous webcrawlers, appearing in Pleistocene profusion."

Interestingly, Sterling also notes: "It's a rather rare phenomenon for an established medium to die. If media make it past their Golden Vaporware stage, they usually expand wildly in their early days and then shrink back to some protective niche as they are challenged by later and more highly evolved competitors. Radio didn't kill newspapers, TV didn't kill radio or movies, video and cable didn't kill broadcast network TV; they just all jostled around seeking a more perfect application."

What is key, he says, is "what kind of personal relationships we forge with the many worlds of media, how we use it, how we insure that we are not used by it." He also makes the following observations:

- Media is an extension of the senses.
- Media is a mode of consciousness.
- Media is extra-somatic memory. It's a crystallization of human thought that survives the death of the individual—generates simulacra. The mechanical reproduction of images is media.
- Media is a means of social interaction.
- Media is a means of command and control.
- Media is the means of civil society and public opinion.
- Media is a means of debate and decision and agit propaganda.

All true and, as ideas, all worthy of debate and discussion

The media-consuming public seems to have an unlimited appetite for new media. It is not just technologies that die, but our relationships to them. With more to watch and more to experience, attention spans shrink, diverting our attention away from programming that asks us to care about our society in one way or another. Sometimes those programs are perceived as boring. I used to be a heavy TV watcher. I am no longer. As it dumbed down the news, I began looking elsewhere for more trustworthy sources. Media addiction is no longer a conscious means to an end, if it ever was; today it is a road to a lack of consciousness. News was always a part of the "boob tube" that made a claim to offer edification. No longer.

Increasingly, even as the mainstream media gets slicker, the public that we've been told likes what it sees, is turning it off and tuning it out. We know this from surveys that span the political spectrum—far fewer viewers are watching network news programs and far fewer readers are buying newspapers. But these surveys are rarely reported and even more rarely dwelt upon. (In July 2005, several TV networks were demanding Congressional action against rating services like Nielsen because they didn't accept their data on shrinking viewing levels.) The last thing media outlets want to report on is why the public is turning against them. Thus, though the media is designed for "tune-in," tune-out seems to be the trend.

One recent example from a related field: In the summer of 2005, Sony, a major media company, was caught in a pay-for-play scandal, also known as "Payola." As the *New York Times* reported: "The finding that gifts were used to help tailor the playlists of many radio stations comes as audiences show signs of rejecting the music choices made by programmers. The iPod and other portable devices have begun cutting into the popularity of radio, and the growth of satellite radio has been putting pressure on the station owners to play a broader range of music."

This disconnect between what the public really wants and what the TV news programs offer is now leading to anxiety in high places. As recently as July 2005, *Broadcasting and Cable* editor Max Robbins observed, "Almost everyone in the game operates in a state of uncertainty. Believe it. A day doesn't pass by when I don't hear about one of a long list of news executives with big bull's-eye targets on their backs." This volatility breeds demoralization and, often, more risk-adverse programming, because when jobs are on the line its safer to follow the pack rather than innovate. Conformity is often the result.

These media scandals seem to be erupting more frequently than political scandals, and the credibility of major media continues to decline. One Pew Center public opinion poll—in one of those rare moments when members of the public were asked for their views—found that as many as 70% of the people asked expressed dissatisfaction with the media. Nearly 70% were angry, but for different reasons. Nearly half think the media is too left wing—not surprising after years of the Republican Party's punditocracy trashing the so-called "liberal media." The other half blames the right wing for souring them on media, pointing to Fox News and a tendency for big media to defer to big government.

In the general public, there is a growing number of complaints as MSM insiders puzzle over slipping ratings and why young people are abandoning news networks for comedy channels to get their news. In other words, there is unquestionably a growing anti-media attitude in the culture at large at the very time that media institutions seem to be more powerful than ever.

Linda Foley, who runs the Newspaper Guild, a union of newspaper reporters, sees hostility to big media growing. She writes on the media website hearusnow.org: "Across all states and nearly all states of mind, 'the media' have replaced 'politicians' as one of our most reviled institutions.... The days when Woodward and Bernstein were folk heroes and Walter Cronkite was the most trusted man in America are long gone."

Significantly, 70% of the people who work in the media tend to feel the same way as their customers. They know how empty-minded many MSM decision-makers are and how much contempt they have for their audience. Journalists know that they routinely practice self-censorship, opting for stories that appeal to the lowest common denominator. In other words, as anger at the media grows, support for the media plummets. Many of our elections are now viewed mostly through the window of manipulative political commercials not held to standards of truthfulness. There are more pundits on the air than journalists. A trend towards sillier and sillier programming results in a lack of respect for media outlets and the shows themselves.

Part of the reason is the blurring of lines between facts and opinion, news and entertainment: Reality on TV is being replaced by "reality-based" programming. Some of these shows are even promoted as educational when they show people of different races interacting with each other or living together harmoniously, something we rarely see on the news. A study in England praised the *Big Brother* show for promoting racial tolerance. Reality shows are often seen to be spontaneous and unscripted but are, in fact, as tightly formatted, controlled, and managed as any Hollywood fare by casting agents, script doctors, and show runners. This is why the staffers that make the shows want the same union representation that sitcom employees enjoy.

This genre has its own star system and there are even reality shows about reality shows. For example, cable TV network E! has announced a new program called *Kill Reality*, which, as the program's blog puts it, "joins together television's most infamous cast members from your favorite reality shows and invites them to take a shot at one another—and another 15 minutes of fame—while finally getting their shot at the big time—by starring in an all-new horror film, *The Scorned*."

It is not surprising that one of the most famous comments about television was Newton Minow's phrase classification of it as "a vast wasteland," a land where trivia rules, gossip lives, and we will be right back after the next commercial break. It is also an industry that has proven itself resistant to change, perhaps because of its deeper and darker nature, summed up by the late Hunter S. Thompson: "The TV business is a cruel and shallow money trench, a long plastic hallway where thieves and pimps run free, and good men die like dogs. There's also a negative side."

CAN THE SYSTEM BE CHANGED?

One way to renew a failing system is to bring new players into it. Can new owners get into the American media mix with new programming? In some instances, they have. Mega-web portals like Yahoo and Google are newcomers. Fox News has only been around for ten years, although it's not exactly the kind of media I would be hoping for, even as it has demonstrated that there are other ways of presenting news and information.

But in all of these cases, it took capital, often from wealthy entrepreneurs with access to the means to compete. Some have been idiosyncratic, like Ted Turner who was never able to translate his "mouth from the South" affinity for unconventional ideas into programming. Others, like Rupert Murdoch, introduced tabloid techniques long practiced in Britain and his native Australia. And there are still others, like former Vice President Al Gore, who is starting a new cable channel, Current, to give voice to the hopes of younger viewers; and Air America, a fledgling radio network trying to bring progressive voices into a talk radio universe long dominated by the hard right.

More challenging perspectives will largely be frozen out of the market as long as the present constellation of power remains. The leading public interest organization that monitors and lobbies on communications policy, the Consumers Federation of America, studied this problem of market entry, too, concluding: "There has been almost no entry into the business of publishing daily newspapers, the mainstay of print journalism, in decades. The record shows that the number of papers and owners has been shrinking, not expanding. Entry into the TV business has also not taken place at the level of ownership. Although the number of full power stations has increased, the number of owners has declined sharply."

Without wider media ownership, variety in programming will continue to shrink. We have yet to come up with a way to create public policies that encourage new entrants into a media business in which production of programs is much easier to create than it is to distribute. This has been done on a small level to encourage more minority owners in broadcasting, but even they have often been funded and controlled by larger media entities. More diverse ownership in itself will not necessarily stimulate the kind of innovation that is needed. New formats and approaches are required.

Revitalizing the news takes fresh blood, yet young people are leaving traditional journalism and developing other news sources. Merrill Brown, a journalist who has run many media outlets, issued a report for the Carnegie Corporation concluding "the future of the U.S. news industry is seriously threatened by the seemingly irrevocable move by young people away from traditional sources of news...." Participation by younger people in political movements and community-based campaigns testifies to their interest in being more than passive recipients of information. Many want to be more involved and are major consumers and users of new technologies that permit them to do so, such as cell phones, video blogging, podcasts, websites, digital cameras, and even video games. There are also new software technologies, including open source software, that are creating new platforms for more interactive information sharing and expression in the realm of current affairs.

These software applications cost little or nothing and are seen as alternatives to, and in many ways superior to, products made by large software companies like Microsoft. Using them is often thought of as an anti-corporate gesture. They are easily shared and widely accessible. A whole generation of computer savvy "geeks" know how to hack computers and modify applications.

The Indymedia network used this technology to create a global network of websites that permit easy news uploads by users and visitors. This new generation of media activists have also spawned a network of low power radio stations.

PART II

A SLOW-BURNING "REVOLUTION"

WHO WOULDA THUNK?

"Who woulda thunk?" asked *Washington Post* media writer Howard Kurtz "that so many Americans would care about arcane FCC rule making? I didn't." What Kurtz was talking about was an unprecedented public protest involving three million Americans that, up to that point, had been generally ignored by the media, including by those who are specifically assigned to track such issues, like, well, Howard Kurtz. Now, what had been building for a while seemed so sudden to him, he went on to term it "a revolution." It's enough to summon up a prescient line from Bob Dylan: "Something is happening here, but you don't know what it is, do you, Mr. Jones?"

In any event, the massive protests did not stop the Federal Communications Commission from supporting demands from broadcasters that they relax ownership rules. The Commission, led by Michael Powell, son of Secretary of State Colin Powell, had a Republican majority that voted along party lines. The Congress protested the decision but did not overturn it.

Media activists—including the Prometheus Project, a group promoting low-power radio stations, and others—then took their case to the courts arguing that the FCC had acted unlawfully. To the government's surprise, the Third Circuit Appeals Court upheld the plaintiffs charge. In 2005, the Justice Department said it would not appeal. This does not mean that those interests lobbying for looser rules have given up, only that they were stopped this time by a combination of protest and legal action. In other words, the war was not won, but the battle was.

The battle, and the general lack of attention it received from mass media, points to something that is largely unknown to most Americans: Our communications laws recognize the public interest in media as paramount. The law actually says that the airwaves are owned by the public and that the public's best interests are more important than the interests of broadcasters. In other words, demands for media change have a constitutional basis. This tension between public interest needs and commercial interests has made media a battleground since the early days of broadcast journalism. In radio, for instance, there were regulators who spoke up—often quite eloquently—for the responsibility of broadcasters to our democracy. In the 1920s the Federal Radio Commission, a forerunner to the FCC, wanted to ban all advertising during the prime time 7-10 PM slot. And in the 1940s, as TV emerged, the FCC's then chairman Paul Porter wanted the new medium to unite Americans, saying: "Television's illuminating light will go far. We hope to drive out ghosts that haunt the dark corners of our minds—ignorance, bigotry, and fear. It will be able to inform, educate and entertain an entire nation.... It can be democracy's handmaiden by bringing the whole picture of our political, social, economic and cultural life to the nation." In the end, the ownership of the airwaves matters because what is broadcast over them matters. In the case that challenged the FCC's change in ownership rules—"Prometheus Project v. FCC"—the plaintiff's brief makes this argument. It is worth reiterating here because the principle that the public's interest is paramount has conveniently been forgotten by most media companies and the media outlets that often do their bidding. The brief reads:

> Broadcast media concentration has been a major concern of the FCC since the early days of radio and is central to the agency's mission. The commission is charged under the Communications Act with ensuring 'localism' in broadcast media. It also has an obligation under the First Amendment—because of the limited number of television and radio licenses that can coexist in constrained broadcast spectrum and the importance of information dissemination to democracy—to ensure that broadcasters 'present those views and voices which are representative of [their] community and which would otherwise... be barred from the airwaves.'
>
> The quid pro quo for broadcasters' right to exclusive use of publicly owned spectrum is their commitment under the Communications Act to serve the 'public interest,' because it is 'the right of viewers and listeners, not the right of broadcasters, which is paramount... the right of the public to receive suitable access to social, political, aesthetic, moral and other ideas and experiences which is crucial here.' This 'trusteeship' theory of broadcast licensing has been a pervasive influence on the FCC's regulatory approach to media concentration for nearly 70 years.

Concerned that national radio networks held too much economic power over affiliates and were therefore impeding the diversity and localism objectives of broadcasting, beginning in the late 1930s the FCC sought to control the power of national radio networks. In *National Broadcasting Co. v. United States*, the Supreme Court affirmed the FCC's power to regulate radio networks, ruling that the act's 'public interest' standard is not unconstitutionally vague and that the scarcity of spectrum justifies imposition of public interest obligations on broadcasters.

It is important to know that media rights are enshrined in the law. Having worked in broadcast companies where legal departments police broadcast practices, I know how important it is to have laws and regulations that permit and protect journalists in doing their jobs and embolden media organizations as well.

When I was a radio news director at a large commercial station we all knew that our owners were funding and programming our many radio documentaries and news specials only because the broadcast laws mandated a certain news and public affairs commitment, when those rules were abolished in a wave of deregulation, cutbacks followed. Within a few years, despite listener objections, the News Department itself would be phased out and replaced by a part-time newsreader.

FEAR TO CHALLENGE

Media issues make politicians nervous as well. Many fear that if they question or criticize media, their access will dry up—or, of course, they fear they'll be ripe for a world of new criticism and negative portrayals themselves. But the problem is even more multi-dimensional than that. It involves issues of education and culture. It intersects with the pressures of a consumer society tethered to media as its marketing tool. It raises issues of government policy and regulatory priorities. Should broadcast media—including cable and satellite—have to adhere to public interest obligations, and, if so, what should they be? How can the public lobby for its interests when self-interested media companies dominate the playing field with vast budgets and skilled lobbyists? And what about the conflicts of interests that occur regularly when industry executives and spokesmen end up becoming the regulators?

Nor is the problem unique to the United States. In Great Britain, the Campaign for Press and Broadcast Freedom (CPBF) put this issue at the top of its agenda, writing in their own 2005 manifesto: "The Campaign's concern is that debates about media policy, certainly over the past decade, have been firmly directed and influenced by a range of media corporations and lobbying groups whose primary focus has been to ensure policies favorable to their commercial success and growth. Also the main political parties have accepted that media companies should be encouraged to expand to take advantage of the 'multimedia revolution' and compete with the global media giants like Time-Warner and Walt Disney. The voices of ordinary viewers and listeners, those working in the media, and those concerned about the democratic and cultural importance of the media have been neglected. If we really care about the possibility for truly democratic and diverse media, then the ideas and policy issues in this Manifesto need the widest debate and support."

What seems clear is that Britain is going through what Americans had already experienced: cutbacks in public media, budgets slashed and major layoffs at the BBC, and a growing trend towards privatization. To many who grew up with the BBC—known as "Aunty"—these developments were shocking. What they do point to is how the corporate order is changing thanks to globalization. Trends in a dominant country like the United States quickly spill over into other countries. As the international trading system and WTO impose rules for market access, broadcasting and media giants pursue opportunities to grow their market share abroad. The logic is simple: If the BBC is permitted to broadcast on American cable, then why shouldn't U.S. broadcasters be seen in Britain? And they are.

Add to this the problem of powerful private interest lobbies that try—and too often succeed—to influence politicians to insure their own interests. This has led to the vast presence and extensive power wielded by media companies who contribute to political campaigns and on whom many politicians rely for visibility and influence. Through lobbying and campaign contributions, a global corporate media juggernaut often shapes the rules that the public has to play by.

So when you envision changing the media through political means, you quickly find yourselves up against vast concentrations not just of media, but of political power that is rarely reported on. All the media companies have large lobbying forces driven by well-connected lawyers and former legislators. In the U.S., they also work through the National Association of Broadcasters, a group that can mobilize local stations to put pressure on legislators who worry about criticism in their home districts. Media companies that make campaign donations can also determine which politicians to provide exposure for and which to keep invisible.

And, not surprisingly, this nexus of influence is barely covered in the media. Most newspapers relegate coverage of regulatory issues or corporate consolidation to the business pages, as if the more general reader has no interest or stake in the debate. Meanwhile, many newspaper companies own TV and radio outlets but rarely disclose their interests or conflicts. A *New York Times* editorial, for example, acknowledged that its parent company had been lobbying to relax cross ownership rules—rules that block most newspapers from operating broadcast outlets in their prime markets; the subject has never come up in its news pages.

Sadly, media reform groups cannot match the industry's budgets and staffs. What they need to do is rely on grass roots pressure and generate their own media to raise public awareness of these issues.

WHAT KIND OF MEDIA DO WE WANT?

The first step in making change is to think about what changes are needed and come up with a program that can inspire citizen engagement. We need to articulate what we are against—that's easy. But what are we for? What kind of media do we want? And what are we prepared to fight for?

Many organizations worldwide have been thinking about this very question. In 2003, the UN held the first phase of a World Summit on the Information Society in Geneva to bring them all together. While it didn't accomplish as much as it hoped—few UN sessions ever do—it did put issues of media access, the "digital divide" and media freedom on the global agenda, recognizing these issues as matters of international importance. The UN summit was well attended, with "Nearly 50 Heads of state/government and Vice-Presidents, 82 Ministers, and 26 Vice-Ministers and Heads of delegations from 175 countries, as well as high-level representatives from international organizations, private sector, and civil society."

And why is so much of the world, and especially poorer countries, so concerned about media issues, and so "up in arms?" Because, as the Uruguayan economist and writer Eduardo Galeano explained in an interview with me, they look for news of their own cultures in large media outlets in vain. Many feel that the global media renders them invisible. He said: "Most of the news the world receives comes from and is directed at a minority of humanity—understandably so from the point of view of the commercial operations that sell news and collect the lion's share of their revenues in Europe and the United States. It's a monologue by the North. Other regions and countries get little or no attention except in the case of war or catastrophe, and then the journalists covering the story often don't speak the language or have the least idea of local history or culture."

Galeano may be from Latin America, but his remarks can be applied to the crises in the Middle East and Africa. "News," he observes, "tends to be dubious and sometimes, plainly, simply wrong." And then, he offers this clincher: "The South is condemned to look at itself through the eyes of those who scorn it."

A situation this serious, an imbalance this great, demands some new thinking, planning and imagining—in other words, actions such as those recommended by the UN WSIS. One can also see, in Galeano's argument, how and why many in the world view American media as a force of cultural imperialism and domination. This is, in part, what new regional news channels like Al Jazeera and the new TeleSur in Venezuela are challenging.

While most Americans don't realize it, U.S. media packaging and style is now a global phenomenon. Years ago, when I was at CNN, a new program called *World Report* was launched to give global broadcasters a chance to present the news their way. Diversity was the hope. What happened in practice was seduction and co-optation. Many news anchors from other countries began to ape CNN's style and approach in the belief that it represented "real journalism." A CNN training course for affiliates reinforced this idea. The result: more uniformity of approach and, in the end, of content.

American-style media has become the "international style" as presentation techniques often trump content. And it brings with it the same American-style problems—of top-down corporate control, of lack of diversity, and the absence of citizen participation. Our style of media has become everyone's problem—it's a global issue.

PART III

MANIFESTOS, PROPOSALS AND DECLARATIONS

I DECLARE MEDIA INTERDEPENDENCE

Reforming the media is not a new preoccupation. Over the years, and in many countries, writers, journalists, and intellectuals have debated—often heatedly—about how to create a better media. The result is a rich history of manifestos and policy statements outlining a variety of concerns. An appendix of some recent manifestos is included in this volume.

Studying this history inspired me, in my first book *The More You Watch, The Less You Know*, to issue my own Declaration of Media Independence as a framework for change. The point was to frame a series of principles and demands that a media and democracy movement can champion. I called for a break up of media monopolies and more citizen involvement. The full text of my declaration is also included in the appendix.

Many agreed with the idea of elaborating a broader call for media change. In the mid-90s media activists and alternative journalists organized two Media and Democracy Congresses: one in San Francisco that drew 600 participants, and a subsequent one in New York that rallied 800. Debates were fierce but little was done to implement their recommendations. Unfortunately, in the absence of a structured organization or well-organized campaign, both were essentially talkfests, forums for debate. There was little follow-up or planning for collective action, probably a function of a lack of funding. (Foundations support conferences more than organizing campaigns.)

Something persistent was sparked, however, and today, in 2005, the issues debated at the Media and Democracy Congresses have reemerged on the agendas of numerous organizations, including some new ones working in coalition to promote better media policies. Organizations such as Common Cause, one of the leaders in media reform, and Free Press (formed by Robert McChesney and journalist John Nichols) are building impressive organizations with coordinated campaign structures complete with lobbyists.

Common Cause, with a membership of more than 600,000, previously focused on campaign finance reforms, but decided after the 2004 election to make media reform a top priority, and has aligned with other groups working on the same issue. A statement on the Common Cause website explains that its "immediate priorities" in the effort to "promote public interest obligations for broadcasters" are:

- Getting regulators to agree to impose specific public interest standards on broadcasters, using as political leverage broadcasters' desire for a rule to require cable operators to carry all their digital programming (the "must-carry" rule);
- Continuing our work in Congress and at the FCC for better ownership rules;
- Protecting the independence of public broadcasting in the upcoming congressional reauthorization of the Corporation for Public Broadcasting;
- Developing the policy tools and networks necessary to advance a long-term agenda for media reform that responds to changing technology.

Among the specific challenges the site goes on to outline are: What should happen to analog TV stations when all channels go digital? Should the

FCC set aside more digital channels for public interest channels on satellite and cable outlets? Can the programming on public broadcasting be shielded from interference from aggressively ideological conservatives appointed to top jobs at the Corporation for Public Broadcasting?

Another approach to tackling media reform has come from younger people and activists from communities of color, who see media reform as a social justice issue. Media Justice is their cry. They see media reform in a civil rights context and demand reforms as a matter of equality and fairness for all. They, too, have had summits and have issued manifestos, often laced with the language of hip-hop and the energy of youth. An example from Mediajustice.org:

> The connections between media—its form, content, and who owns it—is inextricably tied to issues of social justice, power, and equity.
>
> As Media Justice organizers, we are part of a long legacy of struggle for a fair and just mass media. From the courageous organizers who stood up for fair television coverage in the 1960s, to the thousands who marched, protested and sat in to challenge media concentration among white owners, people of color are a vital part of the struggle for a free media.

Today, media justice organizers struggle with how to build meaningful participation from communities of color and indigenous communities to take back this important right, to take back our airways, networks, and cultural spaces. We aim to fundamentally change up the structure, language, and discourse on media within our communities, so that communities that are directly affected can own the movement and the vision behind Media Justice. We also recognize the interconnectedness between our literacy as media producers/cultural workers, with the fight for media accountability, and the need for alternative media institutions and networks within our communities.

Therefore, we define the media justice movement to include folks who are working on media advocacy, media accountability and policy, cultural workers and trainers of media production (film, video, radio, etc.), alternative journalism and virtual/real world technology organizing.

We seek new relationships with media and a new vision for its control, access, and structure. And we understand that this will require new policies, new systems that treat our airways and our communities as more than markets. Similar to the Environmental Justice Movement, (a movement that developed to oppose the dumping of toxic waste or the siting of polluting energy plants in minority communities) the organizing body of the Media Justice summit felt that communities of color, indigenous communities, and other working class communities in the U.S. needed to stake out a different space within and apart from the larger media democracy movement in order to better address differences in the focus and approach to our media organizing.

At the heart of this approach is a rigorous race, class, and gender analysis. We were not content to have these issues relegated to one panel or one segment in a very different mainstream discussion. We need our own space so that OUR communities that are directly affected can forge a movement and vision for this work grounded in our reality.

The media justice movement focuses its energy on reaching out to young people in communities of color. It is decentralized and works on the local level, fighting for municipalities to offer free wireless Internet connections, challenging programming on commercial radio stations and the representation of youth crime on TV news. They are articulate, creative, and often very angry, not only with corporate media but also with middle class media organizations that tend to marginalize their concerns and issues.

In Oakland, California, some local groups supported by San Francisco's Ella Baker Center, have successfully challenged the local Clear

Channel-owned music station, demanding better news and more diverse music. In San Francisco, a local campaign was mounted to press local TV news outlets for follow-up on police brutality cases and to stop stereotyping black youth as criminal perpetrators. A campaign of petitions, community meetings, and marches has indeed won some improvements in local coverage.

THE INTERNATIONAL DIMENSION

In 1948, the United Nation's Declaration of Human Rights, initiated by American delegates including Eleanor Roosevelt, proclaimed, "Everyone has the right to freedom of opinion and expression; this right includes freedom to hold opinions without interference and to seek, receive, and impart information and ideas through any media and regardless of frontiers." Yet that right, legitimized by the United Nations on behalf of the "peoples" of the world, has frequently been violated and ignored worldwide, including in the United States.

On MediaChannel.org, Liza Dichter assembled some of the international calls for change that have emerged since the 1980s, calls to move media transformation into the realm of human rights and civic empowerment. Her findings show how people in other countries were debating these issues long before Americans even recognized their existence. Dichter noted that, "While discussions of these issues rarely appear in the dominant media (no surprise there), international coalitions have been working for at least 25 years to describe these public concerns and organize around them. Scholars, activists and members of the NGO community have come together to attempt declarations broad enough for mass support, yet specific enough to lead to action."

But history shows that if media reform campaigns *are* able to get past the gatekeepers of public debate, they should expect powerful opposition.

Dichter continued, "In the 1970s and 1980s, the backlash from the U.S. government following UNESCO's efforts to address global communication rights almost brought down the U.N. When developing nations called for a 'New World Information and Communication Order' (NWICO) to redress global information and technology imbalances, the U.S. media responded in force. 'The American media was dead set against the NWICO, and thus NWICO was dead on arrival,' recalls former UNESCO media liaison Joseph Mehan. 'It never had a chance.' After the United Nations officially abandoned the NWICO approach in 1989, grassroots alliances focused on citizen action. Statements like the 'Peoples' Communication Charter,' with recurring themes of media 'freedom,' 'democracy,' and 'rights,' have circulated in conferences and classrooms, but have rarely moved beyond these select circles."

Subsequently, the UN NWICO initiative became even more unique because it was attacked by American media organizations arguing that because oppressive governments backed NWICO, it threatened press freedom. But more often than not, such reform campaigns and initiatives are simply ignored.

Among the most significant initiatives attempting to render media concerns globally over the last 25 years have been:

THE MCBRIDE ROUNDTABLE
In 1980, after years of discussion in many countries, a group headed by the Irish leader Sean McBride for UNESCO concluded, "[T]he utmost importance should be given to eliminating imbalances and disparities in communication and its structures, and particularly in information flows. Developing

countries need to reduce their dependence, and claim a new, more just and more equitable order in the field of communication."

As to why the effort should be international, the Roundtable said it was because "the firm conviction that communication is a basic individual right, as well as a collective one required by all communities and nations. Freedom of information—and, more specifically the right to seek, receive and impart information—is a fundamental human right, indeed, a prerequisite for many others. The inherent nature of communication means that its fullest possible exercise and potential depend on the surrounding political, social, and economic conditions, the most vital of these being democracy within countries and equal, democratic relations between them. It is in this context that the democratization of communication at national and international levels, as well as the larger role of communication in democratizing society, acquires utmost importance."

THE PEOPLE'S COMMUNICATIONS CHARTER

The People's Communications Charter was launched in Holland in 1999. Its purpose was to unite diverse groups behind a communications rights document that was anchored in the belief that there are unique cultural environments in the world that need protection and support.

PCC's founders call the charter "a first step in the development of a permanent movement concerned with the quality of our communication environment," and say "it is time for individual citizens and their organizations to take an active role in the shaping of the cultural environment and to focus on the production and distribution of information and culture."

Access to media production is a key demand: "In order to exercise their rights, people should have fair and equitable access to local and global resources and facilities for conventional and advanced channels of communication; to receive opinions, information and ideas in a language they normally use and understand; to receive a range of cultural products designed for a wide variety of tastes and interests; and to have easy access to facts about ownership of media and sources of information. Restrictions on access to information should be permissible only for good and compelling reasons, as when prescribed by international human rights standards or necessary for the protection of a democratic society or the basic rights of others."

Much of the support for this charter was organized in academic circles, with many media organizations endorsing it as well. The organizers recognized that a document like this was a necessary, but insufficient, tool for building support on the issue, so they also enunciated what they called a "two-fold approach":

> First, strategic level cooperation amongst NGOs must build common agendas, joint funding proposals and exchange and cooperation mechanisms. Gathering, analyzing, and dissemination of information will be a key aspect of this. Second, concrete cooperation could begin through joint activities of the people and organizations participating in the movement, under the following suggested themes:
>
> Access and Accessibility
> Right to communicate
> Diversity of expression
> Security and Privacy
> Cultural environment

Despite their strong efforts, momentum on these issues was hard to generate. Mostly because political entities—and media networks—gave the issues raised little attention. Similarly, an attempt to form a Cultural Environment Movement (CEM) in the U.S. attracted support from some groups on the political left and media scholars, but could not be sustained in the absence of adequate funding and political support.

THE VALENCIA STATEMENT

In 2000, UNESCO convened a group in Valencia, Spain to come up with a plan for assuring cultural diversity. They called for government action: "Governments should be invited to consider policies necessary to support the diversity of cultural expression. At the international level, there is an urgent need for the negotiation of a new international instrument on cultural diversity to address issues related to cultural products in all their aspects."

But in Valencia, as with the Media and Democracy Congresses in the U.S., there were many good ideas, and proposals were developed that expanded the international agenda, but little follow-up ensued. In part, this was because organizations proposing follow-up could not attract funding—media companies had lobbied in the European Parliament to oppose forming such of Parliament groups; members who made media issues a central concern were challenged. In the end, support was limited to measures that guaranteed cultural diversity and support a European film industry.

THE NEW MILLENNIUM:
SEATTLE AND THE BILL OF MEDIA RIGHTS

With the rise of the Internet, a new media industry was created, full of possibilities to redress the failings of corporate media. This stimulated activist concerns—as the Internet became both a way for them to organize, and a cause to organize around—that the Internet should remain a free and open forum. Thus, in May 2000, 4,000 activists and intellectuals gathered in Seattle. One of the results was The Seattle Statement—a call to protect the Internet as a democratic tool to nurture a vibrant civil society, and to respond to the oppression of globalization by more "informed citizen participation." The Seattle Statement is also included in the appendix.

By 2005, a decade after the Media and Democracy Congresses, activist, civic, and media reform groups have begun meeting together to discuss how media reform could be placed on the political agenda so that it doesn't meet the fate of these earlier attempts. More and more of the people involved in these groups have come out of policy and public interest law backgrounds, and have vast experience championing the public interest against media industry initiatives and self-interested regulator or legislative proposals. Within the movement, there is excitement at the idea that this influx of new blood and experience could make for a powerful coalition.

At a retreat organized by the political reformers of Common Cause that brought together many of these new media activists on St. Simons Island, Georgia in May 2005, I proposed that we articulate a clear vision for the future—and then fight for what we wanted, not just what we *don't* want.

The result was The Bill of Media Rights, conceived and drafted collaboratively by a number of national and local media reform organizations from around the United States during the winter of 2004-2005. The document provides a foundation that lists key principles and values—consistent with the First Amendment and the regulatory concept of the "public interest"—that must underlie all contemporary debates concerning media and communications policy. It is entirely in response to the American situation, and was endorsed by organizations claiming to represent 20 million Americans. The document's greatest potential seems to be as an organizing tool—undoubtedly, there are far more people in support of it than have signed on so far. The full text appears in the appendix along with a list of its many endorsers.

SAVING THE INTERNET

With old media firmly in the hands of giant players or public service bureaucracies, media reformers are beginning to focus their energies on the fight for digital democracy: Saving the Internet and making it more accessible has become a key issue for media reformers because the online world is so much more diverse and seemingly less controlled than other media outlets. Yet there too, battle lines are being drawn.

As Philippe Riviere put it in an article for *Le Monde Diplomatique*, "The Internet is going through a phase of confrontation between the public's demand for autonomy and companies' desire to control their customers. In order to make the elements of this control more palatable, they are dressed up as content." At various conferences of online technologists, warnings are issued that the Internet we know today will soon be as obsolete as black-and-white TV. Why? Because decisions are being made right now about the future architecture of the next generation of Internet usage that could limit access, control information, narrow diversity and, in effect, make us pay for services and information flow that we now access for free.

A fee-based "walled garden" model, á la AOL, is the goal of the telecoms, cable companies and Internet service providers (ISPs), many of whom have merged into media monoliths like AT&T. One insider predicted that in five years there would be only five Internet Service Providers left.

The basic research and development for the original web was funded with tax dollars through the Advanced Research Projects Agency (ARPA) of the Pentagon. It was designed as a network to link researchers and universities but eventually blossomed into today's sprawling, global, consumer, and business medium. In other words, from its inception, the Internet has been a model of how well invested public money can achieve a public benefit.

But private commercial interests are financing the technological development of the next wave of online connectivity, and they have a different agenda, focused, of course, on their own interests, not the public's. These companies are investing billions of dollars into broadband technologies to turn what has been largely an information-based medium into a video-driven shopping mall-like entertainment emporium.

International organizations, dominated by business interests, are already hard at work on new protocols and rules to rationalize and tame the Web. Writer Steven Hill asks, "How many people have ever heard of ICANN, the Internet Corporation for Assigned Names and Numbers? Depending on whose description you read, ICANN is either an innocuous nonprofit with a narrow technical mandate, or the first step in corralling the Internet for commercial and other purposes."

ICANN is a nonprofit corporation that was chartered by the U.S. Department of Commerce in November 1999 to oversee a select set of Internet technical-management functions previously managed by the U.S. government. In theory, a nonprofit can do the job as well as the government, but not if it's dominated by private interests and lacks accountability and transparency. Notes Hill, "Their functions include fostering competition in the domain-name registration market (i.e., the selling of .com, .net, and .org suffixes) and settling disputes over 'cyber squatting' (the intentional buying of domain names like McDonalds.com for later resale at exorbitant prices to the corporation)."

Sound benign?

Except that ICANN has operated secretly, with its very existence unknown to most Internet users. The reason is simple: It is not being covered in the media. Real News Network in Canada recently aired an expose that showed how little coverage ICANN has received in the international news outlets. The tongue-in-cheek report compared coverage of ICANN to coverage of actor Tom Cruise. It was no contest; Cruise citations overwhelmed ICANN citations 95-1. The real "mission impossible" here seems to be getting the news media to focus on the interests behind what could be an attempt to not-so-virtually steal the Internet.

Elsewhere, corporations are insisting that they own the underlying technology of the Web (even though it was the Pentagon that funded its creation) and want to get paid by those who use it. British Telecom, for example, is claiming to have the patent for the hyperlink technology that is at the heart of the Internet's interface. Can you imagine having to pay BT a nickel every time you click on a link? Don't laugh. It could happen. This battle is wending its way through the courts.

These convoluted claims and counterclaims will keep lawyers and judges busy for the rest of the millennium. And don't assume that just because corporations want to do something they'll be able to. Many of the biggest dot-com-ers, despite their impressive business plans and "revenue models," are operating on shaky ground. The Internet boom and bust in the U.S. is a case in point. Billions of dollars were lost.

Open access is one of the key issues in the battle over whether big companies will control the next generation of the Internet by excluding content they disapprove of or by making it too expensive for smaller users to use. Advocates of internet freedom argue that conduits—the people who own the transmission equipment and cable—should operate like phone companies and not regulate content in any way. Already a federal judge in the United States has ruled against groups who want to preserve open access. As MediaChannel.org reported, an appeals court in Oregon has overturned an open-access ordinance in Portland that was upheld by a lower court last year. Community groups in Philadelphia and other communities have been campaigning for municipal wireless services as a way to assure that all citizens, regardless of income, can take advantage of digital communications. In Philadelphia,

Comcast, the company that controls most online services, is opposing the demand for free Wi-Fi. This issue was among the most discussed at the 2005 St. Louis Media Reform Conference, with many organizations vowing to launch local campaigns for free Wi-Fi as a way to promote media and democracy concerns.

The Center for Digital Democracy's veteran activist Jeff Chester wants the Federal Communications Commission to take a strong stand in this matter in order to preserve the diversity and democracy that have long been hallmarks of the narrowband Internet, and to insure that the broadband lines of the future will be open and competitive. They have convinced *The New York Times*, *The Boston Globe*, and *The Los Angeles Times* to support them editorially, but the cable companies resist. This is because, as Tony Wilhelm of the Benton Foundation points out in his book *Democracy in the Digital Age*, the cable companies need to "recoup their investment in the upgraded infrastructure" and "corral viewers into the net of advertisers." If they are successful, says Wilhelm, "citizens will be less likely to navigate noncommercial, civic environments online."

The key question is: What will the FCC do if and when the issue comes before it? DSL networks, used by telephone companies to provide speedier Net service, are governed by open-access requirements because they are provided by telecoms, which are regulated. Shouldn't the new broadband providers in the cable industry have the same requirements? If they don't, the argument can be made that not-for-profit civil-society and NGO sites will have a harder time finding audiences because they won't be available through cable modems, the prime delivery vehicle for broadband technology.

In June 2005, the Supreme Court ruled that cable companies are not required to share their high-speed Internet broadband networks with rivals. This ruling is a blow to more access for what Jeff Chester calls an "online civic sector—for networks that serve as effectively as they sell" which is, he notes, "something that we've needed all along."

However, those of us who want democratic remedies to prevail have more than big corporations to worry about. Democracies thrive on public participation in political affairs and civic involvement. With all its faults, the media system stimulated interest in social issues and choices. It brought the country together through coverage of political events and national tragedies, like the Kennedy Assassination and the 9/11 attacks. That still happens, but with so many channels competing for public attention the audience and public is increasingly fragmented. The decision by all the networks not to offer gavel-to-gavel coverage of national political conventions fed an erosion of interest in politics.

And now, according to research from the Center for Information Policy, Americans are abandoning the idea of being part of a greater civic body for home-centered private lives— consuming more and more customized media along the way and packing their personal environments with all manner of personalized information technologies. For example, young people get their music from iPods, not the radio, and many of us prefer getting our news on the Internet rather than watching it on TV with family members. As family sizes shrink, as more and more people live alone, the idea of robust civic forums shrinks as well. Add to this the "digital divide" that is an aspect of the growing gap between the wealthy and most working people—and to some degree the young and the old—and you get an idea of the problems in promoting media equality via the Internet. The challenge of providing online access to all is a big one, and not easily solved.

Civil rights activists are worried about this too, as well they should be. David Honig of the Minority Media and Telecommunications Council submitted a brief to the FCC recently that invoked the memory of W.E.B. Dubois' prediction at the beginning of the last century that the defining issue of the 1900s twentieth century would be "the problem of the color-line." The defining issue of this century, says Honig, is "the information line—the institutionalization of two societies, one information-rich and one information-poor." Honig and the MMTC are going beyond demanding rights of access to asserting a "media participation right" intended to reflect the ways in which consumers use media in their daily lives—that is, as participants in the creation and transmission of content, as recipients of that content, and as respondents to that content.

An added danger is the growth of government surveillance—the monitoring of our information—alongside the growth of vast data bases that catalogue all of our choices. Some of these are operated by commercial companies in order to track our reading and buying preferences. Others are run by government agencies in the name of national security. Provisions of the USA PATRIOT Act, for example, required librarians to track what their patrons read and provide information on their interests when asked by agencies like the FBI. What's more, they were not allowed to reveal to the patrons they were under such scrutiny.

In short, the fight for privacy needs to go public.

PART IV

PUBLIC BROADCASTING VS. THE PUBLIC

INDEPENDENT FILM AT RISK

Many media activists have come to invest hope in the growth of the independent film movement. "Docu-democracy" has been on the rise, with numerous indie films and documentaries revolutionizing our media system.

2004 was called the "year of the documentary" by many media writers. Michael Moore's *Fahrenheit 9/11* demonstrated that there is a large global market (half a billion in box office sales to date) for dissenting perspectives that can compete for the mainstream moviegoers' attention. And at Sundance and other worldwide film festivals, I even realized an amount of success that surprised me with my own film *WMD: Weapons of Mass Deception*.

But beyond the proliferation and success of compelling, well-made films—*The Corporation*,

Control Room, Hijacking Catastrophe, The World According to Bush, Bush Family Fortunes, and *Out Foxed*—there is a deeper meaning to this phenomenon that directly impacts the media and democracy fight. This explosion in documentaries is part of the emergence of an oppositional culture responding to the decline in quality in our media system—the uniformity of its approach to news and information, and the growing distrust it has spawned.

Meanwhile, scholars and critics are debating its potential. American University's Pat Aufterheide says the documentary explosion "emphatically shows what it takes to cut through the data-smog (as David Shenk terms it) of our overheated mass culture. We're all info-overloaded, and put-upon. Emotion and attitude cut through." Kevin Lally, editor of *Film Journal*, says: "Multiple factors may underlie the surge in political pop culture. The ownership of mass media by giant conglomerates makes independent film one of the few places where criticism of corporate chicanery can reach a large audience."

Leaders in the film industry are betting on it. Philippe Diaz, of Cinema Libre Studio, which distributes many of the leading documentaries, thinks: "People will tell you that five or ten years ago they never would have thought to go to a documentary in the theater, but because now they are so disenfranchised by what they see on TV in terms of news, they will go to theaters to see a documentary movie."

The spread and popularity of film festivals worldwide also testifies to the growing public interest in connecting with the other visions and voices provided by documentaries. They have created a platform for screening independent films, and also a venue for film-goers to interact with film makers by asking questions, taking part in panels and voting on films in competition. Having spent months on this circuit showing *WMD: Weapons of Mass Deception* at festivals in Nantucket, Boston, Los Angeles, Chicago, Denver, Dallas, and overseas in Copenhagen and Amsterdam and other locations, I had the opportunity to interact with thousands of people from all different backgrounds who packed screenings and participated in a way that the traditional media does not permit—in Q& A sessions and informal settings that encourage conversations and criticism.

The growing number of film students and media programs is another sign of interest in a broader media transformation. Increasingly, concerns about the media system are part of media education. At one of the festivals I attended, the

International Documentary Festival in Amsterdam (IFDA), there were also panels, "talk shows," and master classes. And the IFDA provided a link between young documentary filmmakers and industry professionals. There was also the IFDA Forum, where filmmakers could pitch their work to commissioning editors from TV stations and discuss their work with colleagues. This makes for access to distribution in a way that filmmakers rarely encounter when they have to go one-on-one with TV buyers and others, who often have prejudices as to what they will and will not look at in the first place.

Of the 250 films shown in Amsterdam (out of 2,500 submitted), few will ever be seen on American channels. American TV stations prefer a lowest common denominator of reality shows, lifestyle and wildlife films, rather than hard-hitting programs that might turn some interest groups off or alienate an advertiser. This has led to a risk-adverse environment where even wildly popular movies like *Fahrenheit 9/11* are censored and suppressed by tightly controlled TV stations despite the films' proven success in attracting audiences. And unfortunately, public television in America is sometimes even more tepid and conservative than its commercial counterparts.

Documentary films will not change the world, but they can, and do, raise awareness, and inspire us to realize what is possible and worth fighting for. And one thing that would help filmmakers is less opposition and inhibiting costs from a restrictive rights culture. Copyrights controlled by big media outlets make it harder and harder for independent filmmakers to gain access to affordable footage. A disapproving big media can deny use of material when it doesn't agree with a project's point of view, or it can demand high commercial fees that put footage and music out of the reach of most low budget filmmakers

For example, there is the case of one of America's best-known historical public television series, *Eyes on the Prize*, a highly regarded documentary about the American civil rights movement. The acclaimed award-wining series can no longer be screened because the music copyright owners refuse to renew music licenses, making them prohibitively costly. Filmmakers pay for these rights usually for an initial TV run. These licenses have to be renewed and the license holders can jack up the costs. Usually film budgets cover initial costs of making a movie, not insuring its availability in the future.

Filmmaker Peter Wintonick, director of *Manufacturing Consent* and other films, calls on all media workers to promote the new digital revolution. He calls for a fight against the "apocalyptic, mega-media locusts: Old Hollywood; Old Fictive Fantasy; Old Reality; Old News; Old World; Old Vision; Old Inhumedia; Old Disembodied Corporate Dreams." He wants to engage us all in a "multi-logue" not a monologue—by encouraging more filmmakers to work collaboratively. This means that media makers also have to become media activists, supporting organizations and unions fighting for more diverse filmmaking and exhibition spaces.

There are many ways media makers can work together to cross-promote each others' work—sell each other stock footage at affordable prices, cooperatively buy insurance and marketing services, etc. The public can help too with more funding for filmmakers and by demanding that film companies distribute independent films and that TV channels show them. Usually, people write to the media when something pisses them off. It's time to write to support work you like and to demand more. When I was a network producer, it was very helpful to be able to point to expressions of support for certain kinds of stories and approaches.

FIGHTING FOR PUBLIC BROADCASTING

Independent filmmakers have a stake in revitalizing our public broadcasting sector. The power of the BBC, and many public service broadcasters in other countries, shows how a gutsy public sector can win audiences and contribute to a robust democratic debate by screening documentaries and other programs with independent perspectives. Independent filmmakers are often shut out of commercial venues. They depend on public media for access and support. Unfortunately, our own public broadcasting service, PBS, is fighting for funding and autonomy. It is among the most risk adverse of broadcasters because of government scrutiny and the need to attract corporate underwriting and support.

Bill Moyers is among the best known producers and personalities on PBS. His work has been featured prominently for decades. Now he has become one of the most outspoken critics of public broadcasting. At the National Conference on Media Reform in May 2005, he blasted the Bush Administration for appointing to PBS and to its funder, the Corporation for Public Broadcasting (CPB), ideological conservatives who are out to cleanse PBS of dissenting perspectives.

Moyers also acknowledged that the problem went much deeper than just the people at the top. He cited studies that show how conservative PBS had become institutionally *before* the recent spate of right-wing appointments at the CPB:

> . . . extensive research on the content of public television over a decade found that political discussions on our public affairs programs generally included a limited set of voices that offer a narrow range of perspectives on current issues and events. Instead of far-ranging discussions and debates, the kind that might engage viewers as citizens and not simply as audiences, this research found that public affairs programs on PBS stations were populated by the standard set of elite news sources.
>
> Public television all too often was offering the same kind of discussions and a similar brand of insider discourse that is featured regularly on commercial television. They just weren't so noisy. Who didn't appear was also revealing. In contrast to the conservative mantra that public television routinely featured the voices of anti-establishment critics, the studies found that alternative perspectives were rare on public television and were effectively drowned out by the stream of government and corporate views that represented the vast majority of sources on our broadcasts.

The so-called experts who got most of the face time came primarily from mainstream news organizations and Washington think tanks rather than diverse interests. Economic news, for example, was almost entirely refracted through the views of business people, investors and business journalists. Voices outside the corporate Wall Street universe, non-professional workers, labor representatives, consumer advocates and the general public were rarely heard.

Public TV reformer Jerry Starr of the Committee for Independent Public Broadcasting says that attacks by conservative groups on PBS have gotten results. Writing on MediaChannel in 2005, he noted that conservative funders were successful in getting their shows on the air: "PBS has a long history of capitulating to pressure from conservative Republican politicians egged on by right wing advocacy groups.... In 2002, writing for *Current*, the public broadcasting trade paper, former CBS and ABC news correspondent Jerry Landay revealed that three conservative foundations—Bradley, Olin, and Scaife—subsidized at least 17 programs or series on PBS over the period 1992-2000. All the programs served as 'a platform for the views' of the foundations' grantees and their organizations."

This indictment certainly mirrors my own experience working in PBS stations and submitting programs to PBS for distribution. Two series we produced at Globalvision were rejected by PBS—in one instance because " 'human rights' is an insufficient organizing principle for a TV series." (Unlike cooking or home improvement shows which have sufficient "organizing principles.") And in another instance, our *South Africa Now* series was not considered of wide public interest and "not corporate friendly," to quote one programmer. The shows did get on the air, but we had to find independent distributors and approach stations individually.

I am a media critic who is also a media maker, and I am eager to blast some holes in the media system that will help more diverse work to be seen. And like many independent filmmakers in an environment characterized by increasing homogenization and the disappearance of what some programmers used to call "dissenting documentaries," it's not so easy to do. Commercial pressures have not only tightened things up at the big networks, they've affected noncommercial broadcasters such as PBS, too.

"PBS has been forced to rely increasingly on corporate sponsorship and support in Congress from across the political spectrum," observes documentary filmmaker Fred Glass, whose *Building the House They Lived In* chronicles the California labor movement's successful fight for fair employment practices in the 1950s. "The more PBS is perceived as promoting programming of the left, such as labor history, the less certain it is to receive the support of the right." And I would add that it's not just the right that withholds support. PBS stations, fearing attack for a lack of balance, suppress controversial fare themselves.

Unlike many other countries where public service broadcasting is still strong, if at risk, PBS doesn't offer much of an ongoing cultural or political alternative. Filmmakers critical of mainstream points of view are shut out of commercial TV for all intents and purposes. For them, PBS is often the only game in town. Their only shot to get their work seen by the widest possible audience is to get it on PBS's national program service—what is called the "hard feed"—because that guarantees all public stations nationwide will carry it. (To clarify, PBS is not a network but rather a programming service that supplies a primetime lineup a few nights a week to affiliated public television stations. For their other time periods, locally run PBS stations acquire, and occasionally produce or finance, their own shows.)

If the keepers of the PBS gates turn you down, you can still get your show on the air, but you have to try to sell it, or more likely place it for free, on a "soft feed" that gives individual stations the discretion to run it or not. This can mean it'll be on at different time periods, or not at all, making a national promotion campaign very difficult. You have to lobby station by station across the nation, like a beggar selling his wares.

What this means is that the stations set up to provide an opening for ideas denied in the rest of the media system are also often closed. The fifteen member Carnegie Commission, created in 1965 by the Carnegie Corporation of New York, released its report, "Public Television: A Program for Action," on January 26, 1967, which articulated a mission for public television that has largely been abandoned, including a call to insure that PBS would be a "forum for debate and controversy."

It said: "The programs we conceive to be the essence of Public Television are in general not economic for commercial sponsorship, are not designed for the classroom, and are directed at audiences ranging from the tens of thousands to the occasional tens of millions."

A POLITICIZED PROCESS

The programming selection process at PBS is driven by politics and personalities and internal conflicts. As Bill Moyers once told me, "If you think the war in the Balkans is bad, imagine what would happen if the PBS stations were armed."

Internally divided, uncommitted to any alternative vision, and dominated by a culture of conservatism and caution, PBS opts for safe programs even as some on the right relentlessly frame it as an outpost of communist propaganda. (Was it something that Big Bird of *Sesame Street* said or Chef Julia Child cooked?) That false image, exemplified by slogans like "if not PBS, who?" clouds the real content of their often tepid and frequently recycled programming.

The torpid bureaucracy helps to maintain that status quo. Filmmaker Kevin McKiernan echoes a common frustration among documentarians proposing programming to PBS. Not only was it difficult to communicate with stations, but internal decision making works against the network's founding principals. McKiernan finally heard that "Oregon Public Television liked the film but informed me that 'stories with a foreign element no longer fly' at PBS national." As this implies, there has been an ongoing and longstanding pattern of exclusion of dissenting perspectives. That's why producers and critics who believe that PBS was put on earth as a forum for controversy and debate, a place to present ideas that get screened out by the commercial monoliths, have been battling with PBS for a generation. At bottom, these disputes are about politics and values, not technique or temperament. The problem is that for many producers, if PBS says no, it is hard to find anyone to say yes. So it also is probably not a wise career move to question the process or—Big Bird forbid—protest, because then you are marked as a troublemaker.

Meanwhile, PBS is at risk of drifting even further rightward. As Globalvision's Rory O'Connor noted on his "Media is a Plural" blog: "So if you've been appalled [that]...millions of taxpayer dollars were lavished on a public affairs program anchored by the soft-right son of a former chief of the Corporation for Public Broadcasting (CPB), and a news chat show featuring the hard-right editorial board of the Wall Street Journal...horrified by the selection of the former head of the Republican National Committee as CPB president...and were moved to call for CPB Chair Ken Tomlinson to leave his post...watch out! You're about to get what you asked for. The controversial Tomlinson's second one-year term expires in September—and he cannot be reappointed. Who is replacing him? None other than the former head of the Republican Party, Patricia Harrison."

An overly complicated system does nothing to ameliorate this. With PBS being a program service that only supplies a few nights of national programming, and with the Corporation for Public Broadcasting overseeing the entire structure and passing along federal funds on a selective basis, the system is decentralized, with most program decisions occurring at the local level. And many of the local affiliates are controlled by local businessmen, educators, or bureaucrats. There is, in the end, little public participation in public broadcasting.

All of which is why TV's Public Broadcasting System is losing programming genres to commercial cable stations across the dial. (Something similar is happening at National Public Radio, also part of the Public Broadcasting System. NPR has made enemies by battling low-power, low-range stations run by local producers, while the Pacifica Foundation radio network, also a public network, is fighting internal battles that have on a few occasions become so heated that they have actually brought out the police.)

And all of which is also why public television viewing is dropping steadily. According to Jerry Starr, of Citizens for Independent Public Broadcasting, in a speech at the Chicago Cultural Policy Center on December 1, 2004: "Between fiscal years 1993 and 2002, public TV memberships declined by 20 percent, from five million to four million," and since then, "this trend has accelerated." What's more, said Starr, "The loss in memberships reflects a loss in viewers. In 1987, PBS had a rating of 2.7. This dropped to 2.2 by 1992, 2.0 by 2000, and 1.7 by 2002; 37 percent over 15 years and 15 percent in just the last two."

Meanwhile, activists and citizen groups are crying out that public broadcasting in America has abandoned its Great Society-era foundations and is failing its Carnegie Commission mandate to present diverse perspectives. They warn that the CPB has bowed to commercial pressures and corporate influence, because of inadequate funding. Charges of bias abound from both the right and the left. In a media-saturated country and a media-saturated age, can we still seclude some public space from the marketplace?

It is important to note that today public media and the public domain is no longer limited to public broadcasting. And it is important to create more public domains. Patricia Zimmerman, a professor of media studies at Ithaca College's Park School, wrote about this on MediaChannel in June 2005, calling for a new fusion of public media. "We need a popular front uniting all sectors of our public media ecology. We need to intermix and crosswire its heterogeneous elements—media reform, low power FM, high art cinema, PBS and NPR, film festivals, music samplers, archives, radical gaming, video installation, net art, long form investigative documentary, Internet cut-ups, music samplers, cable access, bloggers, and beyond."

It's clear that those of us who want to change the media order have a big job ahead of us. Saving and expanding public broadcasting must be part of that agenda. We need to find better ways to work together—to synergize at the bottom the way big companies are doing at the top—and translate what we know into more effective messages that will resonate with the consumers we want to activate as citizens.

PART V

MEDIA WORLD PERCEPTIONS

THE U.S. MEDIA AND WORLD PERCEPTION

There is a growing gap between how many Americans perceive themselves and their place in the world, and how others in the world perceive Americans. A June 2003 University of Maryland study that polled almost 19,000 from 19 different countries found, "A majority of people in the world do not feel the world is going in the right direction, a view strongly linked to the view—held by a majority—that the United States is not having a positive influence in the world." Related to that, the Maryland study also found that, "A majority views globalization positively, but majorities—especially in rich countries—say that the rich are not playing fair in trade negotiations with poor countries. In most countries the UN is well trusted."

Yet even as studies identify a major gap between how the rest of the world sees "us" and how we see "them," there is still far more interest in the rest of the world among Americans than is reflected in our disinterested media, or among our politicians. (A disinterest exemplified, for example, in the startling fact that half of the members of Congress do not have passports and have never traveled outside the U.S.)

But Americans' interest in the rest of the world warrants little coverage in the mainstream media. One reason for that may be that it points to misperceptions in the media and among political leaders. A new book by authors Steven Kull and I.M. Destler, *Misreading the Public*, examines this phenomenon and asks, "Do American policymakers really know what the American public wants in U.S. foreign policy?" Through interviews with members of the policy community, the authors revealed a pervasive belief—especially in Congress—that, in the wake of the cold war, the public is showing a new isolationism: opposition to foreign aid, hostility to the United Nations, and aversion to contributing U.S. troops to peace-keeping operations. This view of the public has in turn had a significant impact on U.S. foreign policy.

But when the authors tested these assumptions in a national, in-depth poll, they found this to be untrue.

If the data points one way, why do political leaders prefer the other? Pollster Daniel Yankelovich, President and Founder of Public Agenda summarizes their study: *"Misreading the Public*...shows that Americans are not as isolationist, anti-UN, anti-UN peacekeeping, or anti-foreign aid as Washington policy makers believe; it demonstrates that Americans do not approach foreign policy from a narrow what's-in-it-for-us self-interest, but from a deeply moral commitment to our national responsibility for maintaining world peace and well-being; and it nails the fact that members of Congress systematically misread, misinterpret, and distort the public's stance on foreign policy."

If government elites misread the evidence, so do many media organizations which have cut back on foreign news. In June 2005, when Tony Blair's government made a commitment to helping African countries with more aid and debt relief, all of the British channels aired documentaries and special reports on the issues. These programs helped create a climate of national concern in which advocacy groups raised millions, and literally hundreds of thousands of people marched to "make poverty history."

This showed another relationship between media attention and public opinion. Put another way, when an issue is not on TV, it doesn't exist in a media saturated country like the United States. When Globalvision produced a series on South Africa's fight for democracy, we were repeatedly told that the public would not be interested. And yet, the program rated well. We found that people can be interested in programming that is interesting in its approach.

This leads to what Groucho Marx used to call "the hundred dollar question": Why? Why do these misperceptions persist? Wouldn't politicians benefit by responding to what the public really wants and believes? The answers to these questions take us beyond the realm of contested issues and bi-partisanship into the often sub-rosa worlds of interests and ideology. But clearly this also points to a massive media failure—the failure of news organizations to cover the world more perceptively and in greater depth, to help Americans understand the issues of concern to the rest of the world. It may be that policy makers prefer that the public not be made aware of underlying problems since questions about their own government's policies and commitments are soon to follow.

The failure of coverage actually keeps the public in the dark when the coverage that is given lacks context and explanation. For example, we see the horror of events in countries like the Sudan and Chechnya without much background or reference to the role of oil or economic interests. Media analysts have documented similar gaps and omissions in coverage of almost every major military or political conflict. Did the U.S. invade Iraq in order to gain access to its oil reserves? Some government officials have denied it, but the media has a duty to explore the issue rather than ignore it or accept government claims at face value.

What is happening in the world is important to our economy and security. Americans are extremely diverse, with many different connections to the greater world—from the Mid-western farmers who export grain, to the many companies that do business in China.

Sadly, however, our media is not doing all it could to keep that diverse population informed about their role in global issues. In a global age our world is increasingly interconnected and interdependent. America is not and cannot be an island unto itself. Those interconnections are seldom shown, nor, for that matter, is the work of many non-governmental groups who are working to improve the lives of people in developing countries. It is not just "bad news" that's missing. Positive stories are also in short supply.

In a political and media system riddled with deceptions there is a tendency among politicians and journalists alike to conform to a dominant narrative, to be unwilling to question the conventional wisdom even when it is blatantly wrong. Nowhere can this be seen more clearly than in the coverage of the Iraq war. Most Americans don't know that, as President Bush vows to build a safer world, much of the world says they fear him more the characters he hopes to defeat.

COLLUSION

While making *WMD: Weapons of Mass Deception*, a film about the media coverage of the war on Iraq, I learned that virtually all American media outlets boosted the war. One study cited by Greg Dyke, the former head of the BBC, found that of 800 "experts" on the air during the run-up to the war, only six opposed it.

Fairness and Accuracy in Reporting (FAIR) confirmed those statistics. In a study of U.S. war coverage published in their magazine, *EXTRA*, they found "the guest lists of major nightly newscasts were dominated by government and military officials, disproportionately favored pro-war voices, and marginalized dissenters." FAIR's study, which started the day after the Iraq invasion began, March 20, 2003, and ended three weeks later on April 9, looked at 1,617 on-camera sources used for war coverage on the six major evening newscasts: ABC World News Tonight, the CBS Evening News, NBC Nightly News, CNN's Wolf Blitzer Reports, Fox News Channel's Special Report with Brit Hume, and PBS's NewsHour With Jim Lehrer. It found that "Official voices dominate: 63% of all sources were current or former government employees. U.S. officials alone accounted for more than half (52%) of all sources."

New York Times columnist Paul Krugman contrasted U.S. and British coverage, charging that U.S. outlets "behaved like state-run media." (British media did better, but even there, critics found a pro-war imbalance in the main news bulletins.) Geneva Overholser, a former ombudsperson at the *Washington Post*, now with the Poynter

Institute, agrees. "The comments I've been hearing about U.S. media becoming ever more like state-run media seem to me to evoke something deeper than partisanship or ideology," she said on Poynter's website. She also writes: "What I sense is a narrowing of the discussion, an echo chamber of conventionalism. Sure, we have the appearance of controversy, what with our shouting heads and sneering pundits. But real debate—substantive representation of viewpoints not currently in vogue, of people not currently in power, of issues not currently appearing in our narrowly-focused eye—is almost absent."

This total lack of balance on the screen concealed an unreported confluence of issues behind the scenes. It is a case of collusion, even complicity, between broadcasters and the Pentagon. There, in the "patriotic correctness" of post-9/11 America, TV anchors and newscasters had largely accepted the credibility of U.S. government claims. In the absence of any skeptics or alternative views, they surrounded themselves with experts from Beltway think tanks, Pentagon officials, and retired military officers.

Many crossed the line from journalism to jingoism, talking in terms of "we" as if the networks were fighting the war. They bought into the logic and inevitability of pre-emptive war, rarely challenging its skewed assumptions and flawed "intelligence." As one unnamed editor of the *Washington Post* explained after his paper and the *New York Times* issued modified *mea culpas* for their slanted coverage, "what's the point of raising these points, the war is going to happen."

At the same time that all this pro-government "reporting" was going on, behind the scenes, media companies were lobbying the FCC for rule changes on media ownership to benefit their own bottom lines. They wanted rules that would allow them to own more TV stations, and to permit newspapers to buy stations in their principal markets. These rule changes would allow big companies to get bigger, consolidate their influence by controlling markets, and become even more profitable. The question was raised: Did the FCC agree to waive their rules if the media agreed to wave the flag? This sounds like a crude accusation when in fact it simply seems to question what's obvious, and speaks, as well, to the common you-scratch-my-back-I'll-scratch-yours way business is done in Washington, where special interest lobbyists often wield real power. This relationship being questioned involved the media, and was, of course, not covered by the media. It was a blatant conflict of interest that was never acknowledged.

In *WMD*, Jeff Chester of the Center for Digital Democracy made the charge outright: "The reason the coverage, in part, was so tepid, was so timid," he told me, "was because these same media companies like News Corp., Fox, GE, NBC, Viacom, CBS, were trying to curry favor to win the support of the Bush administration for this huge give-away on media ownership."

U.S. Congressman Maurice Hensche went further, explaining: "This is not something that happened yesterday. It didn't happen over night. It has been going on here in the United States for about two decades at least. And it's been a process— it's been an organized, concerted, thought-out, well planned, and well-executed process, going on back to the Reagan administration, flowing through the first Bush administration, and now being picked up successfully so far by the second Bush administration. This is a plan, it's a plan, it's not serendipitous, and it doesn't happen accidentally, it's what they want. They want to be able to control the political discussion."

And sometimes "they," the big media companies, have more direct interests at stake as well.

General Electric, the company that owns NBC and other cable channels, won $600 million in contracts to aid in the "reconstruction" of Iraq.

THE RISE OF THE "MEDIAOCRACY"

What such stories-behind-the-story illustrate is that the reasons we see what we do—or alternatively, do not see what's important—is that there are often unexamined or hidden interests at play.

While the networks, for example, followed the speeches at the Republican National Convention in New York for the 2004 Presidential nomination, journalist Bill Moyers took his cameras to the glitzy parties. There, defense contractors entertained and saluted the members of Congress who had held power over government contracts and appropriations. His reports on PBS got closer to the truth of what was happening in our government than all the hoopla and hype of the RNC on the other channels. And the mainstream media's coverage of the Democratic convention was similar—never looking closer at the inner working of power.

Mediachannel's Media for Democracy campaign monitored the election coverage in its entirety. MediaChannel's Tim Karr reported: "Data, compiled for MediaChannel.org by international media monitoring firm Media Tenor showed that in January the three networks devoted less than 5 percent of their coverage of the Democratic campaigns to the candidates' positions on the five election issues that Americans say matter the most."

Election coverage has a dynamic that goes largely unchanged year after year. Just like in the war coverage of Iraq, there is a "master narrative" driving the reporting. The 2004 master narrative revolved around the dirty swipes back and forth between the Democrat and Republican campaigns, a process made simple for journalists by a coterie of campaign operatives on hand to deliver the latest jab in the form of talking points, spin, and counterspin. Major campaigns today operate as if they are at war, with extensive media monitoring operations of what is on all the channels and then what the opposition is doing. These units are often based in what party operatives call "war rooms." They have professionals studying all the coverage in real time, 24/7, and then cranking up "rapid responses" when warranted, by handing out special releases, position papers, and other forms of "spin." In this war zone, the media becomes the battleground.

It's not clear if the Pentagon learned its media techniques from campaign operatives or vice versa. Tommy Franks, the U.S. war commander revealed to a journalist from the *London Telegraph* that during the war his desk had five TV sets on it. One showed what every news channel was featuring, changing every five seconds. Information dominance was a goal of the media war Franks was fighting alongside the military conflict. Shaping the coverage was a priority. Old style PR techniques gave way to sophisticated perception management strategies. What is true in media's relationship to armed conflict today is also common in political conflict.

It is widely assumed that our media operates outside the political system as a watchdog, a "fourth estate." But in the Iraq war Franks assigned the media a role in his war plan as "the fourth front." The role of the media had changed. The Pentagon actually adopted Hollywood narrative techniques to emphasize story telling rather than sloganizing or even traditional briefings, like the ones run by General Norman Schwartzkopf during the Gulf war.

What the Pentagon realized is what political campaigns have long practiced: create a narrative built around heroic stories driven by key messages and constructed events. In many ways this is an adoption of the successful soap opera paradigm in current affairs and news. As media scholar James Wittebols explains in his book, *The Soap Opera Paradigm*, news presentations now rely on entertainment formulas. He explains:

"A 'live' presentation can enhance the vivid emotion present in a story and make viewers feel closer to those involved in a story .... Seriality in news stories helps present a continuing character development that may encourage viewers to see 'good' and 'evil' sides in stories portraying conflict."

This is partly why networks promote intense partisanship, believing that it is heat, not light, that sells. In a medium in which wrestling is one of the most popular program formats, it's not surprising that political programs are set up as fights, often between cultural archetypes who are masters of hurling invectives and putting each other down. The clash of ideas is more important than any resolution or explanation.

These problems have been particularly acute in the U.S. in the aftermath of the 2004 election year, when many in the media portrayed the country as bitterly split between 'red' and 'blue' Americans. Mainstream media have become divided as well—Republicans watch Fox News, Democrats watch CNN. And the rest of us have tended to drop out.

This perception of a polarized nation and media persists to this day. But rather than work to find common ground among Americans, mainstream media are fueling the divisiveness. The few massive corporations that dominate the modern media landscape boost profits by portraying an America at conflict with itself, and with the rest of the world.

For example, shouting pundit programs—including MSNBC's *Hardball*, CNN's *CrossFire*, Fox News Channel's *O'Reilly Factor* and the since cancelled CNBC's *Dennis Miller Live*—favor partisan jousting over a substantive debate of issues. The private purpose of such on-air confrontation is to drive ratings up and maximize shareholder value. But this hyper-competitive profit making often stands at odds with the public need for balanced journalism and diverse perspectives.

The most prominent example is surely the emergence of Fox News Channel. A network that achieved ratings success by promoting partisan and abrasive news celebrities has spawned an industry-wide shift from hard news towards hyperbole and "infotainment." Talk radio, from Rush Limbaugh to Air America, has also championed on-air news "talent" who push the envelope with comments meant to divide—and even offend—Americans. It's profitable, but is the public well served by news outlets projecting opinions rather than presenting facts and useful information? Mustn't we do better?

Opinion is now more prevalent than reporting. There are three times as many pundits on the air as journalists, and in universities, three times as many students study public relations than study journalism. Recent surveys of young people show a profound lack of knowledge about the First Amendment and even hostility towards it. There is a growing lack of respect for traditional media, according to a survey released in January 2005 by the University of Connecticut. There is now a consensus of complaint where there used to be admiration and faith.

All around us lie the fault lines of an industry in profound turmoil—what many are calling a "post-journalism" period, where mainstream media reporting is more about packaging, posturing and profit-making than about information sharing. But the rise of the privatized big media news industry, with its controversy-driven reporting and opinion, has sparked a public backlash. In many instances, politicians become pundits and pundits politicians. Jerry Springer was a big city Mayor before he became the host of a TV interview program that featured physical fights on the air.

Tim Russert, George Stephanopolous, and Chris Matthews were all political functionaries before becoming journalists. It's a circular world where politics and media meet and meld.

Media today is an integral part of the political process, a key component in what I call our "mediaocracy." The rise of this "mediaocracy" is not the result of a crude conspiracy nor is it an accidental occurrence. Its roots can be found in the intensifying corporate media environment that has been changing for years, as well as in the increasing corporatization of politics itself.

It reflects a growing symbiotic relationship between increasingly interlocking media elites and their political counterparts. Together they form a powerful interdependent system in which overt ideology and shared worldviews mask more covert subservience to corporate agendas. Together these two forces form a "mediaocracy"— a political system tethered to a media system

After every election, journalists do post-mortems acknowledging their own limits and mistakes. The honest ones admit there was a uniformity of outlook in which the "horse race" and scandals are over-covered and the issues are under covered.

They concede that there was a focus on polls without explaining their limits adequately or how polls in turn are affected by the volume and slant of media coverage. There are criticisms of how entertainment values infiltrated election coverage, what *Time* magazine calls "Electotainment." They bemoan the fact that there was more spin and "opinionizing" than investigative reporting. These *mea culpas* are sometimes a form of confession and self-cleansing for journalists. For institutions, they are a credibility buying exercise signaling that they still maintain certain journalistic ethics—so please don't turn that TV off, don't drop your newspaper subscription yet, we know, we know we've been bad.

Months after the election, the *Capitol Times* in Madison, Wisconsin summed up the consequences of this type of election coverage in a pithy phrase: "If we had a better media, we'd have a better president."

PART VI

WHAT CAN BE DONE?

UNITED WE ALREADY STAND

So what can be done to end the decline in hard news, the growth of infotainment, and the continued implication of highly concentrated media owner-ship? How can we convert our media system into a diverse platform for more diverse expression and informed debate? How can we work to insure that media serves democracy? And how can we continue to promote and project media awareness and reform into the future so it all doesn't happen again?

There is no question that the public is open to, if not totally supportive of, media reform. As already noted, a 2003 Pew Foundation poll found that 70% of the American public was dissatisfied with the media, and that 70% of people in the media shared that dissatisfaction.

When Lou Dobbs asked his CNN audience in late 2003 if "big media companies should be broken up?", 5,000 people responded and a whopping 96% agreed that they should be. That is quite a high response from a TV show audience. Nearly three million Americans—from both the right and the left—wrote to Congress and the FCC to protest new rule changes that would make for media ownership in fewer hands. Congressional offices were flooded with email and phone calls. It showed that these issues have traction when organizers campaign on them. It also demonstrates that well organized and marketed campaigns for media reform can win support across the left-right divide.

A media and democracy movement is needed, and is now bubbling up from below worldwide—with parents calling for a more informative way of rating TV shows to safeguard their children, teachers promoting media literacy, activists asking for corporate accountability, consumers demanding enforcement of antitrust laws, media watchers critiquing news coverage, critics seeking more meaningful program content, producers creating alternative work, and independent producers agitating for better and fairer journalism. The public is more aware of the issues and is willing to get involved.

The media problem is not, at its heart, a partisan one—it's about interests, not issues. Reforms can't be based on slogans because they have to try to transform structures.

THE MEDIA AND DEMOCRACY MOVEMENT

Democracy is messy, and democratizing our "mediaocracy" will require engagement. We must work to find common ground that unites Americans who, despite their diverse views, are concerned about the media's role in our society. It will be hard but it can also be fulfilling and fun. One way forward is for all who want a better media to rally around an omnibus concept—what I call a "Media and Democracy Act."

This is why I believe we need a comprehensive approach, an umbrella strategy that can translate what we really want into a legislative package that many different constituencies can sign onto, with the idea that unity is better than disunity.

My idea: A "Media and Democracy Act" that would include proposals for an anti-trust program to break up media monopolies; a funding strategy for public broadcasting and the independent producing community (perhaps financed with a tax on advertising); reinstatement of an updated fairness doctrine; free broadcasts for political debate across the spectrum; limits on advertising and monitoring for honesty and accuracy; guarantees for media freedom in the public interest; media literacy education in our schools; provisions for free wireless; media training and access centers; more support for media arts, etc.

This list is endless. No one group has the clout to put its priorities on the agenda without support from others, so why not make everyone a shareholder in the process? Politics is the art of compromise. That's why a Media and Democracy Act that incorporates all these concerns can have appeal across the partisan divides of politics, as well as the political divides within the media and democracy movement. In its depth and breadth it can actually inspire the necessary compromise.

It will take legislative attorneys, of course, to write such a document. Nor will it be something created alone, like the legend of Thomas Jefferson writing the Declaration of Independence with only marginal help from others. One purpose of such an Act is not to expect to prevail the first time out, but to show what is needed and is possible, how government policy shapes the regulatory framework, and how national priorities and funding could be used to make a media system that truly serves the public interest and informs our democracy.

A Media and Democracy Act is an idea that can help move this movement. It underscores the importance of working together to make media matter and to show a diverse range of interest groups that we can win if we work together.

It's an idea whose time is coming.

HOW IT BEGINS

"What is to be done?" is the oldest and, ultimately the most difficult of questions facing media reformers and wannabe transformers. At every meeting discussing media this question is raised by people frustrated with, and angry at, big media practices. Many know what they don't like in the media, but few know what is involved in changing it.

Activists need to be educated on this challenge along with ordinary citizens. They need to be encouraged to focus more of their energies on media reform as a key lever to building a more vibrant democratic culture. It is significant that many who belong to social movements focus their energy at railing against the government, especially the White House, and currently the Bush Administration, as if it is the sole repository of all power. They see elected officials as the power wielders, not the people in the shadows behind them whose interests they serve. In an age of globalization when real power and resources have shifted from elected officials to corporate interests, the role of corporate media cannot be ignored because its focus often sets and limits the public agenda.

Although a media and democracy movement is emerging, we must acknowledge that it still is seen as a sidebar or even an afterthought to the vast number of groups that are active in political campaigning and fundraising. To them, media is just a complaint, not really an issue. Many are afraid to "alienate" media commentators for fear that they will be branded as extremists of one kind or another and be pushed out of the limelight. They want their "fifteen seconds of fame," to quote Andy Warhol, and are wary of taking on the very interests they depend on for exposure.

Some activists in Howard Dean's failed presidential campaign say his fortunes as the front-runner soured immediately after he called for checks on media concentration. Media outlets don't like it when their practices are called into question. They often point to the fact that they are criticized from both the left and the right as proof that they are doing their job.

This response is non-responsive, because the dissatisfaction with media runs deeper and wider. As already discussed, many polls show that media reform has non-partisan appeal. When the FCC was imposing new rules permitting more media consolidation, nearly three million Americans wrote to oppose it. Nearly half of the critics were from the right. On this issue the National Rifle Association and its critic Michael Moore found themselves both on the same side.

What seems clear is that legal initiatives for media change have to go hand-in-hand with other lobbying and pressure tactics. Organizers need to mobilize constituencies. Educators need to galvanize students. Many educators are pushing for media literacy classes in schools so children are more equipped to deal with the media onslaught

Communicators have to educate the public, and political movements and leaders need to put media issues on legislative agendas. We need a "full court press" on these issues, to borrow a term from basketball. This will require persistence, not posturing. And it will take time. Think post-partisan. Think marathon, not sprint.

EVERY CITIZEN A REPORTER

The concern about media concentration and the failures of "balanced" reporting has led to the rise of the media-reform movement—led by such organizations as MediaChannel.org, Common Cause, Consumers Union, Free Press, and others— as people find new ways to wrest control of media back from the corporations. Increasingly, news consumers want to participate in our media, not just be passive recipients of its output. Concepts like citizen journalism are now on the agenda. Blogging is more popular than ever. The idea of being the media, not just watching or listening to it, is finding many supporters. The byproducts of this movement are more visible and influential than ever before. For example, mainstream journalists such as Dan Gillmor, a former technology reporter for *The San Jose Mercury News*, and Rebecca McKinnon, formerly a CNN reporter, decamped from traditional newspaper and broadcast outlets to try their hand at "distributed journalism," devising public websites, blogs, and news services that encourage citizens to take a larger stake in reporting and commenting on the news. Gillmor defines "distributed journalism" as "any project that can be broken up into little pieces, where lots of people can work in parallel on small parts of the bigger question and collectively—and relatively quickly—bring to bear lots of individual knowledge and/or energy to the matter." He sees the possibility for this collective journalism to pool the resources of many participants and cover larger stories than might ordinarily be possible.

Gilmor is a newsman with a mission. As he puts it, "I have interests beyond politics and I don't want to be creating something that is partisan. I think there is a giant group in the middle of American politics that knows that things are really wrong in many ways but they don't like the completely polarized left vs. right that was created during the last few years."

Partly, Gilmor's ideas were influenced by what is already happening on this front overseas. Across the globe, citizens are voting for this new media order with their attention spans, eyeballs, and dollars. One successful example is South Korea's *OhmyNews*, a citizen-edited newspaper that became one of the country's most popular. Now marking its fifth anniversary, founder Oh Yeon Ho told the *Japan Media Review*: "In Korea, readers' dissatisfaction and distrust with the conventional press had considerably increased, the average citizen's desire to express themselves greatly increased. Thus, on the one hand, discontent with the conventional press, on the other hand, citizens desire to talk about themselves. These two things were joined together. The reason the Internet was highly attractive was that I had little money and the Internet meant launching was relatively easy at first—easier than paper newspapers. So I thought the Internet was the space where a few people who possessed nothing could bring about results using guerrilla methods. I thought up our motto, slogan, or concept—'every citizen is a reporter.'"

Ohmy has evolved into a major media force and was even credited with the election of a president when the newspaper crusaded against an unpopular incumbent and helped bring him down. In the United States, similar experiments are underway. The infrastructure for more citizen journalism is already largely in place, with community wireless networks springing up in towns and cities across the country—local and independent broadband alternatives to Verizon, Sprint, and the handful of other telecom giants.

The "Blogosphere" gained new prominence and wider acceptance as a new breed of citizen Web publishers supplemented, and sometimes surpassed, mainstream print and broadcast news outlets in a variety of contexts—from presidential politics to media criticism to real-time coverage of global disasters. This is also true in publishing. The independent company publishing this book, Melville House, grew out of one of the first publishing industry blogs, MobyLives.com.

The emergence of such media alternatives has raised new questions about the vulnerability of Big Media in an era of more interactive and citizens-powered journalism. Can corporate media, designed largely to control the content pipeline and serve the bottom line, ever respond to a public seeking more involvement in news and information? Can media built on a legacy of corporate mergers ever be truly fair or balanced? Can framing every issue as a partisan argument really serve the larger political discourse about solutions to society's problems?

I believe that in order to help nurture more democratic reforms, we need to help encourage a common ground—beyond partisanship—upon which Americans can hold diverse perspectives but agree, for example, to challenge media concentration. Remember that the recent battle with the FCC against relaxing their ownership rules led to the National Rifle Association and NRA critic Michael Moore fighting on the same side! It can be done.

At MediaChannel.org, one of the media organizations I am involved in, we are trying to urge a return to core principles. Below are some of those principles that, as media reform efforts gain momentum we would hope to see other media outlets embrace as well:

Post-Partisan—When there is public disagreement over the nature of a specific media problem, we should consider the issue from multiple perspectives, with writers providing reporting and diverse critical analysis that pulls together the best ideas from all sides of the spectrum. These reports should focus not on opinion, but instead, on uncovering the truth behind the pressing media issues of the day.

Solutions-Focused—Our approach is to derive post-partisan solutions from this larger community—reflecting a far more constructive approach than simply canonizing or demonizing one side against the other.

Forward Looking—As we move into the digital age, it is crucial to understand the array of new technologies that will redefine the way Americans interact with media. With the advent of ubiquitous broadband, low-power FM radio, digital TV, community wireless networks, media-on-demand, mobile podcasting, cell-phone photography, and other interactive media, we are dedicated to the principle that all citizens have the right of access to, and the right to speak in, the public sphere.

Non-Commercial—Media does not, and will not, skew simply to the left or the right. Most allegedly "objective" news coverage today is actually driven by bottom-line commercial and corporate interests that pander to "infotainment" and sensationalism. Free from such considerations (its non-profit status would ensure a lack of commercial bias) media has great promise.

Activism-Enabled—We encourage our colleagues to report on issues and problems, but also to seek and advocate solutions. This activism will be expressed in a number of ways, ranging from creating media to formulating and advocating media policy, from upholding industry standards and best practices to direct contact, constructive criticism and dialogue with media producers and distributors.

BECOMING THE MEDIA

In the end, all of this comes back not to what some abstract *they* will do but what *we* as individuals, acting alone and through our organizations, networks and communities, will do. Will we make media matter as an issue and an obligation? Will we heed the words of the experts and activists who have been telling us that changes need to be made, and can be made?

I was struck, during the coverage of the death of Pope John Paul II—one of the major media moments of 2005—by the irony of the revelation of the Pontiff's dying wish. It seemed to go over the heads of most of those "covering" a spectacle that went on for a week, and, indeed, it was barely reported on. But what preoccupied the Holy Father as his body gave out? What great passion came to him?

He expressed it in his last apostolic letter: It was about the media.

John Paul expressed several wishes as he called for a greater sense of social responsibility *in* the media, and *for* the media, too:"Promote justice and solidarity according to an organic and correct vision of human development by reporting events accurately and truthfully, analyzing situations and problems completely, and providing a forum for different opinions. An authentically ethical approach to using the powerful communication media must be situated within the context of a mature exercise of freedom and responsibility, founded upon the supreme criteria of truth and justice."

He also spoke about media ownership: "I would like to recall our attention to the subject of media access, and of co-responsible participation in their administration. If the communications media are a good destined for all humanity, then ever-new means must be found—including recourse to opportune legislative measures—to make possible a true participation in their management by all. The culture of co-responsibility must be nurtured."

And so, even the Pope understood the importance of transforming our media, even if those whose job it was to cover him missed his passion on the subject. Unlike other papal passions, however, implementing this one does not rely on faith alone—it requires practical steps.

Changing our media demands action and ideas on many fronts, including the legislative, regulatory, institutional, and educational. It's about changing structures of power and ways of looking at the world. It demands thought about what we want from ourselves, not just others. It requires a new consciousness among those that make media and those that consume it.

At a time when so many are dissatisfied with our "lame stream media," to quote one prominent conservative, many are turning inward as well as outward for solutions. A new "personal democracy" movement has emerged where more and more people are not just turning off the mainstream media but turning themselves into a new type of media.

In the late nineties, the activists of the IndyMedia movement launched with the mantra: "Be the media." That call is being realized by as many as ten million bloggers world wide. Not all are journalists of course, but all are creating media. The phenomenal appeal of blogs has inspired audio and video counterparts from podcasting to "user media" on the Internet. A media revolution is underway spurred by new technologies and possibilities.

Media institutions are encouraging "citizens' journalism" as a way to tap the ideas, observations, and energy of ordinary people and involve their customers as never before. This is not only a way of democratizing the media but also of enlivening it. Can an elite, top-down model be replaced by a more populist bottom-up approach? Is this too idealistic or impossible?

Look at the growth of talk radio, and the proliferation of websites, including search engines like Google—which may virtually replace libraries for many people. There's been the meteoric growth of the blogosphere and the emergence of thousands of video activists making programs for public access or showcasing films and documentaries at festivals worldwide. Scholars and writers are contributing to first-rate publishing projects like the Wikipedia, a new online, non-commercial, encyclopedia that taps the expertise of researchers and writers worldwide. More and more citizens' media watch groups are springing up.

We all have to be interested in not just what's wrong with our media system, but in how to make it right. That will take time and effort. It will require fighting special interests and experimenting with new forms—forms that may not all work out. It is a post-partisan fight and a fight that all of us can find a way to get involved in. Here are a few ways to join in:

TEN STEPS ON WHAT TO DO

1. Become conscious of the power of media in shaping our political agendas. Recognize the importance of learning more about its impact, and why media has to become an issue in all social change work.
2. Educate members of organizations, churches, community groups, and social movements about the media dimension of an issue. Hold forums. Invite speakers. Show films. Link your websites to media action groups.

3. Join Media Reform movements to lobby the government and media companies for less concentration of media ownership, and to establish more diversity on the airwaves. Familiarize yourself with the legal and political complexities of the issues and campaigns to break up media monopolies. Let your own local politicians know where you stand on the issues.

4. Campaign in your communities for media literacy education in schools and community programs. Educating young people on becoming critical viewers and readers is essential. Involving younger people in the building of coalitions is a critical component for success.

5. Don't hesitate to provide feedback to media outlets with phone calls, letters to journalists and managers and editors. Submit articles or take pictures of newsworthy events and join citizen journalism initiatives.

6. Support independent and alternative media outlets. Make sure your organizations and schools know about the range of online resources, websites and forums.

7. Participate in public access and public broadcasting opportunities to get your messages out to the public. Develop communications plans around the issues you care about, frame the language that best expresses your concerns and goals and then phone in to call-in shows on TV and talk radio. Lobby city and municipal governments to provide public access TV centers and broadband services.

8. Hold local film and media festivals, for all communities and all ages, to expose your neighbors to the wide range of independent documentary filmmaking.

9. Become the media—develop media-making skills including video, photography, and websites. Democratizing media is not just about what they do, it's about what we do.

10. Do what you can to provide financial support to media organizations that you like. If you want a say you have to pay to keep media alive and independent, because that is too often the kind of media that is struggling for survival.

Obviously, this is all just a start. But if it's true that "we get the media we deserve," it's also true that we get the media we fight for.

If we care about our democracy, can we afford not to act?

America's media consumers are being short changed and many know it. They understand that information is the currency of democracy. They know we can do better and so can our media institutions. And they actually can do something about it.

It's time to do so.

APPENDIX

BILL OF MEDIA RIGHTS
2005

PREAMBLE

A free and vibrant media, full of diverse and competing voices, is the lifeblood of America's democracy and culture, as well as an engine of growth for its economy.

Yet, in recent years, massive and unprecedented corporate consolidation has dangerously contracted the number of voices in our nation's media. While some argue we live in an age of unprecedented diversity in media, the reality is that the vast majority of America's news and entertainment is now commercially produced, delivered, and controlled by a handful of giant media conglomerates seeking to minimize competition and maximize corporate profits rather than maximize competition and promote the public interest.

According to the Supreme Court, the First Amendment protects the American public's right to "an uninhibited marketplace of ideas in which truth will prevail" and "suitable access to social, political, esthetic, moral and other ideas and experiences." Moreover, it is "the right of the viewers and listeners, not the right of the broadcasters, which is paramount."

But too often, our nation's policymakers favor media conglomerates' commercial interests over the public's Constitutional rights, placing America's democracy, culture, and economy at risk. Instead, guided by the principles that follow, policymakers must ensure that the Constitutional rights of present and future generations to freely express themselves in the media, and to access the free expression of others, using the technologies of today and tomorrow, are always paramount.

MEDIA THAT PROVIDE AN UNINHIBITED MARKETPLACE OF IDEAS

The American public has a right to:
- Journalism that fully informs the public, acts as a government watchdog,
  and protects journalists who dissent from their employers.
- Newspapers, television and radio stations, cable and satellite systems, and broadcast and cable networks operated by multiple, diverse, and independent owners employing a diverse workforce.
- Radio and television programming produced by independent creators that is original, challenging, controversial, and diverse.
- Programming, stories, and speech produced by communities and citizens.

- Internet service provided by multiple, independent providers who offer access to the entire Internet over a broadband connection, with freedom to attach within the home any device to the net connection and run any application.
- Public broadcasting insulated from political and commercial interests that are well funded and especially serves communities underserved by privately owned broadcasters.
- Regulatory policies emphasizing media education and citizen empowerment, not government censorship, as the best ways to avoid unwanted content.

MEDIA THAT USE THE PUBLIC'S AIRWAVES TO SERVE THE PUBLIC INTEREST

The American public has a right to:
- Electoral and civic, children's, educational, independently produced, local and community programming, as well as programming that serves Americans with disabilities and underserved communities.
- Media that reflect the presence and voices of people of color, women, immigrants, Americans with disabilities, and other communities often underrepresented.
- Maximum access and opportunity to use the public airwaves and spectrum.
- Meaningful participation in government media policy, including disclosure of the ways broadcasters comply with their public interest obligations, ascertain their community's needs, and create programming to serve those needs.

The American public has a right to:

- Television and radio stations that are locally owned and operated, reflective of, and responsible to, the diverse communities they serve, and able to respond quickly to local emergencies.
- Well-funded local public access channels and community radio, including low-power FM radio stations.
- Universal, affordable Internet access for news, education, and government information, so that all citizens can better participate in our democracy and culture.
- Frequent, rigorous license and franchise renewal processes for local broadcasters and cable operators that meaningfully include the public.

LIST OF ENDORSERS

Acadiana Open Channel
ACME-NorCal
Action Coalition for Media Education
AFL-CIO
Afro-Netizen
AFT 1521
AIA
Akaku: Maui Community TV
Alaska PIRG
Alliance for Communications
  Democracy
Alliance for Community Media
American Federation of Television &
  Radio Artists
American Federation of Musicians of the
  United States and Canada
American Legion Post 315, San Francisco
Arizona Consumers Council
Arizona PIRG
Association of Independent Video
  and Filmmakers
AWARE
Bard College-Annadale Movement
  for a Free Media

Benton Foundation
Berkeley Community Media
Bird Street Media Project
Boots: The Anthology
Brennan Center for Justice
Brunswick Cable 7
Cafe Latino Radio TV
California National Organization
  for Women
California PIRG
CATV
CCTV Center for Media & Democracy
Center for American Progress
Center for Digital Democracy
The Center for Media and Democracy
Center for Creative Voices in Media
Center for Community Media and
  Global Studies
Center on Media and Society
Centre for Society
Centre Media Values
CFI-Florida
Chicago Consumer Coaltion
Citizens for Independent Public

Broadcasting
Common Assets
Chicago Media Action
Columbia College Democrats
Common Cause
Communications Workers of America
Community Media and Technology
    Program, UMass Boston
Community Media Center
Community Technology Organizing
Consortium
Community Technology Centers' Network
Community Television of Santa Cruz
County
Computer Professionals for
    Social Responsibility
Computers In Our Future—SBCC
Consumer Federation of America
Consumers for Auto Reliability and Safety
Consumers Union
CSUAC
CTSG - Carol/Trevelyan Strategy Group
CUWiN
Dallarel Consulting
Davis Community Television
Deep Woods Technology Inc.
Democrats.com
Department for Professional Employees,
    AFL-CIO
Digital Creator Crop.
Dissent=Freedom
Donald McGannon Communication
    Research Center
Durango Community Access Television
Edmonton Small Press Association
Emmas Dance
Epic
Equinox Life Services
Erskine College

FightBigMedia Meetup
Fight Terror Network
Film Arts Foundation
Florida PIRG
Fox Valley Peace Coalition
Free Press
Free Speech TV
Fresno Free College Foundation
Future of Music Coalition
FUUCSA
Gold Star Mothers
Goode Media Services
GR Institute for Information Democracy
Hawaii Public Access Media
High on Adventure
IATSE Local 412
IBEW
Incite Pictures, Cine Qua Non
Independent Online Distribution Alliance
Independent World Television
Indian Online Journalsim
Indiana@Work, LLC
Industry Ears
IndyMedia
Ithaca College Students for
    Media Reform
J. Beauchamp Productions
JEL Management
Kasch Associates
KHENLP
KNFS FM 89.1 Tulane
KQRP-LP 106.1 FM
Latino Print Network
League of United Latin American Citizens
Lifeguard Adventures
LinkTV
Linux Public Broadcasting Network
Lost Horse Press
Lowell Small Business Administration

Lowell Telecommunications Corporation
Loyola University Chicago
LPCTV
LTC
Macalester College Department
  of Humanities and Media and
  Cultural Studies
Massachusetts Consumers Coalition
Maui Citizens for Truth and Justice
Media Access Project
Media Alliance
MediaChannel
Media Democracy Legal Project
Media Empowerment, UCC
Media for Democracy
Media Giraffe Project
MediaRights
Media Working Group
MetaBrainz
Michigan Peaceworks
Midwest Center for American Values
MMCTV
NABET-CWA
NALIP
National Black Media Coalition
National Hispanic Media Coalition
National Video Resources
National Voting Rights Institute
Neighbors Broadcasting
NEK-TV
New America Foundation
New Jersey PIRG
New Mexico Action Coalition
  for Media Education
New Mexico Independent Media Center
New Mexico Media Literacy Project
Newshare Corp.
Nomadic Pictures
North Carolina Consumers Council, Inc.

Nosotros
Nuai
Office of Communication of the
  United Church of Christ, INC.
OK2B
Open Sources
Pacifica
Panhandle Community Radio Inc.
Pasadena MoveOn
Peace Now
Pinnacle Group
Portland Roots Music Project
Privacy Rights Clearinghouse
Progressive Faculty Coalition
  of Indiana University
Prometheus Radio Project
Public Access of Indianapolis
Purchase College
Quote...Unquote, Inc.
Reclaim the Media
Recording Artists' Coalition
River Valley Times
SAP Pail Resource
Screen Actors Guild
Scribe Video Center
Share With Other LA and Media
Challenge
SMCDFA
Social Criticism Review
SpeakSpeak.org
Sweeny Associates
Tacenda/WilloTrees Press
Telecommunications Research and
Action Center
The Neighborhood Network
The Newspaper Guild-CWA
The Peoples Channel
ThinkingPeople
20/20 Vision Factory

United Teen Equality Center, Inc.
Universal Child, Inc.
UCLA Center for Health Policy Research
UCLA Chicano Studies Research Center
UDWA
UnCommon Sense TV
U.S. PIRG
Virginia Citizens Consumer Council
Voice of Vashon
VT Chapter of Action Coalition
  Media Education
Threat Dot TV
Tre-State Media Ministry, Inc.
Two Rivers Farm
Video Association of Dallas

Waipahu Community
  Development Center
Waldo County Progressives
WCCA TV 13 "The People's Channel"
Westchester Community College TV
WestSound Community Television
Wisconsin Democracy Campaign
Wolfeboro Pediatrics
Women's Institute for Freedom
  of the Press
Writer's Arc
Writers Guild of America, East, Inc.
Writers Guild of America, West, Inc.
Zeldo Morgan-Mercenary Journalist

DECLARATION OF MEDIA INDEPENDENCE
DANNY SCHECHTER
From *The More You Watch, The Less You Know,* (Seven Stories Press, 1997).

Two documents from historic and successful struggles for democracy have helped me frame my thinking on media independence. One was our own Declaration of Independence, the seminal statement of the American Revolution that gave the grievances of a colonized people eloquent expression. The other, from the modern era, was South Africa's Freedom Charter, adopted at a Congress of the People in 1955, a clarion call for justice that outlined a vision and the principles for a post-apartheid society. Both documents defined in their times and lands what was wrong, and pointed to what needed doing.

So, with a little creative borrowing, I drafted such a document for adoption by the 1996 Congress of Media and Democracy, which appeared in the Congress's final report. I include it here with no pretensions to literary originality, as a working draft for readers to react to, revise, and, hopefully, in part or in its entirety, to put to use.

We declare before our country and the world that the giant media combines who put profit before the public interest do not speak for us. We proclaim this democratic media charter and pledge ourselves to work tirelessly until its goals have been achieved. We urge all Americans of good will, and people throughout the world who want to participate in a new democratic information order, to join with us.

We call upon our colleagues, readers, editors, and audiences to inform themselves and the American people about the dangers posed by the concentration of media power into fewer and fewer hands. We urge that more airtime and news stories be devoted to a critical examination of the relationship between media monopolies and the threat they pose to the spirit and functioning of the first amendment. We cannot have a meaningful democracy unless our media institutions provide reportage, in-depth programming and coverage that reflect a more diverse range of sources and opinions.

We urge our elected representatives to challenge excessive and concentrated media power because it poses a threat to the future of democracy.

We call for an end to all legislation that promotes censorship and corporate practices that lead to self-censorship. We need government to regulate media monopolies in the public interest and to keep our news media and new electronic information highway open and free of the undue and repressive influence of government bureaucrats, excessive corporate branding, and one-note political agendas.

We urge non-governmental groups, advocacy organizations, labor unions, community groups, and all environmental and social justice organizations to make common cause with us in fighting to create more points of access and accountability in our media system; we urge all citizens to interact more with the media in their own communities by monitoring performance, writing letters, calling talk shows, and meeting editors and radio and TV executives.

We are against techno-solutions like the V Chip—and call instead for a "D Chip," a commitment to use media to promote the values of Democracy.

We want more than ritualized, look-alike and think-alike coverage of elections. We want more coverage of citizen participation in civil society, political movements, non-governmental organizations, and community groups. We share the concerns of many parents with the overload of shows that glamorize violence and cheapen sex.

We demand that media institutions in our society increase the participation of minorities and women in all positions in their organizations. Our newsrooms have to stop being among the most segregated institutions in our country. Racism inside the media contributes to the toleration of racism in the culture at large. We urge news organizations to openly audit their performance in this regard and publicize the results.

We further pledge to join and support efforts to stop attacks on labor unions in our media institutions. Media workers must be guaranteed the right to collective bargaining, and to belong to unions if they so choose.

We call on media companies to reduce the growing internal gap between salaries at the top and salaries at the bottom. Fairness and equity in the media workplace is essential.

"We call upon media institutions to explore the values and practices of 'public journalism' so that the media can begin to better serve the needs of the people. We urge them to adopt codes of conduct that rebuild their credibility in the eyes of a public grown cynical, which no longer trusts the media. We call upon the media to promote tolerance and equality in American life.

We call upon U.S.-based multi-national media companies who already generate more than half of their revenues outside the United States to act responsibly in trading with the nations of the world. Many nations already resent the dumping of American programming, however popular it may be in the short run, into their countries. Others deserve a chance to sell as well as buy programming, to have their voices and concerns heard too. They have the means of production but lack the means of distribution. We oppose the growth of a new "electronic colonialism." We want more global sharing of cultures and viewpoints.

We call upon the governments of the world to respect the rights of journalists—which are in danger in many countries—and the right of the people to read and see their reports.

We call for more public funding of the arts and humanities, including documentary programming. We want America to allocate as much money proportionately to support the arts and humanities as countries like Canada, Germany, and England do. We have the money, let us find the will.

We want to put the public back into public broadcasting and create mechanisms for accountability that bring PBS back to its original mandate to provide programming not available on the commercial spectrum. We want to stop the give-away of the public airwaves and the broadcast spectrum itself. The income from spectrum sales should be set aside for public media. The corporate media sector should be taxed to help subsidize the public media so that the notion of the "free marketplace of ideas" has meaning once again. Private companies can lease the airwaves, not own them.

We pledge ourselves to working cooperatively and collaboratively to help bring the media more in line with the values of democracy.

We ask all who share our goals to embrace this declaration and agree to work on behalf of its tenets so that the principles of freedom of the press, which have given America such a distinctive place among nations, will not be compromised and denied because a handful of huge companies and media moguls are in a position to dictate what our country sees, hears, reads and, ultimately, thinks.

THE SEATTLE STATEMENT
2000

- The world is becoming globalized and communications technology is an important part of that process.
- The human race is faced with a multitude of major problems that are receiving inadequate attention.
- Civic society throughout the world has enormous—insufficiently tapped—resources including creativity, compassion, intelligence, and dedication which can help address these problems.
- At the same time civic society is undervalued and threatened.
- Information and communication technology offers enormous potential for civic society for education, health, arts & culture, social services, social activism, deliberation, agenda setting, discussion, and democratic governance.
- Active, informed citizen participation is the key to shaping the network society. A new "Public Sphere" is required.

VALENCIA STATEMENT ON CULTURAL DIVERSITY 2000

1. Cultural diversity deserves to be protected, nurtured and supported throughout the world. International forums and processes, including those focusing on international trade, must respect the need for nations to protect, nurture and support that diversity.

2. Governments should be invited to consider policies necessary to support the diversity of cultural expression. At the international level, there is an urgent need for the negotiation of a new international instrument on cultural diversity to address issues related to cultural products in all their aspects.

3. International dialogue and discussion on the issues of cultural diversity, involving civil society, governments, and industry and all those concerned with the preservation of cultural diversity. The Forum should act through meetings, virtual exchanges, the gathering and analyzing of pertinent global data ("observatory"), publications and other means, and

should establish an interactive Internet website, for, among other matters, online discussions on cultural diversity, signature drives, and to act as a repository for documents and data.

4. The following measures for protecting and promoting cultural diversity should be put forward for further consideration:

   a) National and international regulations may be needed, as appropriate, for the audiovisual industry to ensure cultural diversity in the production and dissemination of audiovisual goods, products, and services.

   b) The audiovisual industry should consider adopting a series of steps designed to foster local production, including the earmarking of funds.

   c) Public service broadcasting has an important role to play in promoting and enhancing cultural diversity through its programming.

   d) The audiovisual industry should consider establishing and endowing a mechanism, including public-private partnerships, through which the production and dissemination of audiovisual services from endangered cultural areas could be supported.

   e) The audiovisual industry should encourage and engage in joint production and distribution approaches between companies of different cultural regions of the world.

   f) The audiovisual industry should be encouraged to form international network services to help disseminate culturally diverse audiovisual products to a wider global audience.

g) The audiovisual industry, governments and international organizations should encourage and support the participation of films, producers and distributors from local and regional cultural areas, especially from developing countries, in international festivals and presentations, as well as the organization of independent festivals of local and regional films from the developing world.

h) Likewise, support should be given to the training of film-makers and producers from local and regional cultures, covering development and distribution strategies, script writing techniques, dubbing and subtitling, promotion and marketing, as well as use of new technologies and the creation and operation of local TV networks.